Creating Balance

[signature]

Oakhill Press
Greensboro, North Carolina

Also by Carolyn Dickson

SPEAKING MAGIC:
Performance Strategies for Winning
Your Business Audience
with Paula DePasquale

Creating Balance

Moving out of CONFLICT into COMPATIBILITY

by Carolyn Dickson

Creating Balance

Library of Congress Cataloging-in-Publication Data

Dickson, Carolyn
 Creating balance: moving out of conflict into compatibility / by Carolyn
Dickson.
  p. cm.
  Includes index.
 ISBN 1-886939-16-0
 1. Interpersonal conflict. 2. Interpersonal Communication. 3. Inter-
personal relations. I. Title
 BF637.I48D53   1997
 158.2—dc21   97–12490
                                                            CIP

For Amanda, Ryan, and Emma

who have a lifetime of relationships to build

TABLE OF CONTENTS

Foreword

Carolyn Dickson has written a clear, practical, easy-to-apply handbook for moving from disagreement to agreement, misunderstanding to understanding, and enemies to partnership in one's relationships. Drawing from her own personal experience, as well as an in-depth study of the nature of human interpersonal communication, she clearly and concisely articulates the principles, processes and techniques for moving from conflict to compatibility.

Her first principle for effective communication is not being aware of the other person, but rather, being aware of one's self. Self-awareness is the key to understanding the essential nature of effective and ineffective communication. Why is this? Because, as Carolyn understands, we take what is within us, and we express it out in the world. Thus, the conflict we have within ourselves is the conflict that we experience and express with others. "I am not a man but a mob," H. G. Wells observed. Abraham Lincoln, in talking about his inner life, said: "You talk about a civil war, there seems to be one going on inside of me all the time. One of these days I may just split asunder and part company with myself."

Carolyn correctly points out that, after becoming aware of our own internal conflicts, we must adopt self-responsibility as a principle. Inner conflict, without self-awareness and self-responsibility, will become external conflict. Implied in the concept of self-responsibility is that one owns one's internal conflict and resists projecting it outward.

When I accept and own my internal conflict, I am now the cause of it, rather than the effect of it. This feels very much like: "the truth will set you free, but first it will hurt like hell." Since, as Carolyn says, conflict is essentially emotional, accepting responsibility initially is very uncomfortable. It's so much easier to pretend in our minds and hearts and guts that "the other" is the cause of the upset. However, once we acknowledge being the source of our own emotional turmoil, we are now in the psychological position to move to the next step, which is self-empowerment.

If I can be big enough to step up to my own dark side—to look squarely and unflinchingly into the eyes of my own demons, then I am in the position to own my own power. Mark Twain stated: "Every man is like a moon, having both a dark side and a light side." Once I am aware of and own my own dark side, I can now extract and transform the power existing in both my light and dark sides, and move to a state of self-mastery in my communication with all parts of my "inner family." Once I am aware of my inner voices, interests, wants, needs, and biases, I can take the final step—technological mastery. As Carolyn accurately points out in this book, good intentions and self-awareness are not enough. She describes many examples of individuals with good intentions and lousy execution that produce lousy results. Hence, once you become aware of the needs, emotions, expectations, and perspectives of your "conflict partner," you must have a communication technology that produces the results you desire and require.

The final step in moving from conflict to compatibility is to learn and follow the six-step process described in this book. From self-awareness comes awareness of others. From self-responsibility comes an emotional environment in which the other person is supported in becoming responsible for *her* feelings and inner conflicts and misunderstandings. From self-mastery comes mastery of the interpersonal communication process by using the six-step process. By taking the opportunity to grow in one's awareness of self and others, and by using the communication technology described by Carolyn in this book, communication with others becomes a daring, creative adventure. Communication with others, especially when there is a potential for conflict, becomes a challenging opportunity to advance in one's understanding of the heart of communication. Communication truly becomes a daring dance that leads to a growth-oriented understanding of what it means to be a human being in a relationship, and in the larger context of community.

I recommend that Carolyn Dickson's book be on the desk of every individual who is concerned with communicating effectively, clearly, and in a way that the other person experiences the intent and focus of the communication as supportive of their purposes and goals.

Tony Andrews-Speed, Ph.D.
Vice President
Farr Associates, Inc.

January, 1997

Preface

Irreconcilable differences. This is the reason couples give for why they separate. It's what bosses say about why employees are let go and what "fired" people say about why they left their last position. Translated into real words, people who have "irreconcilable" differences are caught up in interpersonal conflict, are having great difficulty getting along with each other, and are feeling doomed to continue in this path forever. Arguments that start out as molehills soon become mountains, and the mountains grow to insurmountable heights. Often, however, the mountains aren't as insurmountable as they appear at first glance, and with the right approach, the differences are far more reconcilable than you might believe.

In this book, I have attempted to go beyond the huge body of academic literature surrounding the complex subject of conflict management and give you a simplified, practical approach to dealing with conflict in the commonplace situations faced every day by normal people (insofar as any of us can be classified as "normal"). In other words, what you can say and do in those emotional moments when you are nose-to-nose with someone who seems determined to get the best of you. Over the years, I have developed the *Six Steps to Compatibility* that are described here as part of VOICE-PRO'S *Conflict to Compatibility Workshop*. These *Six Steps* are equally effective at work and in interpersonal situations. They are designed to keep you in charge of your life and out of the role of victim. They are easy to understand but not always easy to accomplish, for they require commitment and perseverance if you are to become skilled in their use.

I have avoided whenever possible the use of words like *adversary, opponent,* or *antagonist,* because, as you will see throughout the book, I have wanted to create a picture of two reasonable, well-intended people who just happen to have differing viewpoints about common issues. *Creating Balance* is not for severely disturbed individuals who engage in violence or other forms of abuse to get what they want. Far more learned professionals than I can offer help on such issues, and I urge you to seek them out if your situation calls for it. Instead, I have chosen to use the term *conflict partner* to designate that person with whom you are trying to build a better relationship. We derive more pleasure from working with partners than with adversaries, so no matter how angry you get, keep the "partnership" idea in mind.

The stories and dialogs I have used as anecdotal examples are based on real life. Some are complete in themselves, while others are composites. Many of them have been contributed by our Workshop participants, and their successful implementations of the *Six Steps* have been exciting to watch and, I hope, exciting to read about. Most names have been changed to protect the identities of clients and friends; however, Chuck, Leslie, Claire, Susan, and Fred Mackenbach are real people. AccuTech is my fictitious model of a compatible organization. If there are other AccuTechs out there, it is my fervent hope that the model fits them too.

Like all writers, I struggle with the gender question. I absolutely refuse to sprinkle a manuscript with references to "his or her goals," and "his or her conflict." I'm also too old-fashioned to embrace the grammatically incorrect compromise of singular subject and plural modifying pronoun, as in, "Everyone must have their head examined." To make it easier on myself and my readers, I sometimes refer to your conflict partner as "he," and sometimes as "she." I've tried my best to keep the references equal in number, but I didn't count them, so forgive me if one gender seems to be favored more than the other.

As you read, you may notice that I've chosen to close chapters in a couple of ways. At the end of the chapters containing steps in a process, like the *Six Steps to Compatibility* or the different tactics of listening, I've placed a summary that ties the pieces together. In other, more informational chapters, I've created a section called "next steps," which will give you ways to put what you've been reading about into action. In other words, information generally leads to action, while actions are summarized with information.

And finally, I want to express my deep appreciation to all those who made this book possible. To the VOICE-PRO staff—Susan Bookshar, Leslie Dickson, Marie Harris, Cindy Pizzuto, and Heidi Weiker—who kept the doors open and the business running smoothly while I took time out to write; to Marilyn Casey, Carol Crawford, George Havens, Katina Jones, Anthony Moore, and Jeff Susbauer, who were gracious enough to read the manuscript, chapter by chapter, and give of their expert opinion and advice; to my family—Chuck, Greg, Beth, Leslie, and Claire—who never failed to point out where, while I might be knowledgeable, I wasn't making any sense; and to all my colleagues, clients, and friends who formed the laboratory in which this book was created. *Creating Balance* is about real people in real situations doing real things. To those real people I send my undying affection and thanks.

1

The Responsibility Is Yours

With hope and dreams of glory, I founded VOICE-PRO in 1984. Late that year, having experienced some success (and a slightly positive cash flow), I hired a young woman to help me in the business. Soon she became far more than an employee; she became a valued associate, colleague, and friend. And for years we got along fine.

Then, gradually, things began to change. Instead of participating in her normal enthusiastic way in the affairs of the business, my colleague withdrew. She became more and more critical of my decisions, and less and less willing to take an active role in making those decisions. She pretty much stayed in her office and sulked. I in turn felt increasing frustration. I pushed her for explanations, laid down new rules of behavior to compensate for her withdrawal, and drove myself and the entire office to new heights of performance, in order to "demonstrate" how I wanted her to behave.

The more I pushed, the more she withdrew; and the more she withdrew, the more I pushed. As our conflict escalated, the results were predictable. The situation worsened, the relationship deteriorated beyond repair, and eventually my trusted and beloved ally left the company. Anger and hurt remained for a long time afterwards.

This book is about conflict. Or more accurately, how you can improve your ability to manage the conflicts that occur in your life. I'm starting with this story about a conflict from my own life because there are two lessons to be learned from it. First, resolving conflict takes more than good intentions. It takes skill. My associate and I had both invested years of our lives in the partnership, and neither of us wanted to see it disintegrate. We knew that our professional success depended in large part on our ability to get along with each other. We were serious students of interpersonal communication. We were beginning to *teach* this stuff to other people. Our desire and good faith were unquestionable. But for all our study and dedication and apparent knowledge of the subject, we were unable to resolve the conflict between us. Because deep down, we just plain didn't know how.

This book is about that "how." How you can say the words and take the actions that build and preserve the important relationships in your life. How you can develop conflict management skills that will enable you to get along with people in even the most difficult situations.

The second point of my story has to do with who's responsible for dealing with the conflict. My colleague was convinced that I was the cause of her problems and if I would do what, in her eyes, I should do, everything would be all right. *She* was just fine. On the other hand, *I* knew that *I* was no different than I had ever been. *She* was the one who had changed. If *she* would just go back to how she had been before (enthusiastic, cooperative, and uncritical), there wouldn't be any problems.

In my consulting work through the years, I've found that this is invariably the case. When I ask people to describe their conflicts and what they think are the causes, it's always the other guy's fault. *He* is argumentative. *She* is always complaining. *They* don't do things the way they should. The finger always points outward.

No room for victims

It's so easy to play the role of victim. When you decide to be a victim, you give up your power to someone else, someone who's louder, or more manipulative, or who has a status position superior to yours. Victims are classic finger pointers. To them, the perpetrator of the conflict is always someone else. The causes of the conflict are "out there" somewhere.

Brenda was readying the monthly financial statements in preparation for closing the books. Checkbooks, receipts, and other papers were strewn across her desk. Intent upon her work, she didn't notice Jane approach until she heard Jane's harried voice.

Jane: *Brenda, are you busy?*
Brenda: *Er . . . not really.*
Jane: *Can you type this for me? I'm in a terrible rush and it's got to be in the mail by noon.*
Brenda: *Well, I guess so. How long is it?*
Jane: (handing Brenda the papers and heading back to her own desk)*It's only about six pages. Gee, thanks, I really appreciate this.*

Later, Brenda fumed, "She does this to me all the time. Couldn't she see that I was busy? It's just like Jane to be so inconsiderate. She makes me so mad I can hardly work with her."

When she was asked later about the incident, Jane said, "Why didn't she tell me she was busy? I could have done the job if I'd had to, but I thought if someone else had time, it would make sense to divide up the work."

Knowingly or unknowingly, victims are willing and active participants in the conflict relationship. Because she expected Jane to notice how busy she was, Brenda saw herself a victim of Jane's aggressiveness. Her inability to respond honestly to Jane's requests actively contributed to the pattern of conflict that had come to define the women's relationship. Jane dumps the work on Brenda; Brenda resentfully does the work; Jane dumps more work and wonders about Brenda's resentment; Brenda does the work and steams—and the beat goes on. For Brenda to take charge of her relationship with Jane, she must find a way to be both understanding of Jane's situation and openly honest about her own responsibility to get the books closed on time. From Brenda's point of view, the only person who can manage the conflict is Brenda.

Pointing the finger inward

The reality is that we can't change other people, no matter how much we want to. No matter how much they need changing. No matter how much they're disrupting the way we lead our lives and the way we do business. The moment we try to make another person change, he'll dig in his heels and resist with all his might. In any relationship, patterns of behavior are set up that tend to repeat themselves, over and over again, much like a dance. The "finger-pointing method" of conflict resolution says that it's up to the other person to break the pattern. Then if and when that happens, we'll be happy to dance along to the new step. However, if we wait for our partner to take the lead, the dance is unlikely to change, and we'll bumble along as always, forever stepping on one another's toes.

A much better way is for *us* to change *our* behavior, to interrupt the dance by altering our steps. We're likely to experience some stumbling around at first. But if we're steadfast in our resolve, we'll gradually draw our partner into a new pattern, and eventually we'll have begun a new and more satisfying dance.

Fred Mackenbach is the retired president of The Lincoln Electric Company. For me, Fred Mackenbach is the perfect role model for anyone who wants to build satisfying, long-lasting personal and professional relationships. His philosophy is a simple one. "Carolyn," he told me one day in my office, "I am responsible for the success of each and every one of my relationships."

That day in my office, Fred went on to give me an example of how he lives this philosophy day in and day out. "Because I travel so much," he said, "early mornings often find me at the airport. I discovered long ago that the way I'm treated by the skycap can make a difference in how my day goes. If the skycap is friendly, I'm off to a good start. If the skycap is grumpy, it can color my outlook all day. Well, I can't afford to take that chance. It's *my* responsibility to make the skycap want to be nice to me, so I make sure I'm nice to him first. If we both enjoy our 6:00 AM conversation, we both have a better day."

A simple philosophy, yet profound. One that requires skill and great determination to accomplish. And a lifetime of attention. Fred Mackenbach has enjoyed a brilliant career, a highly successful personal life, and the love and respect of everyone who knows him. His philosophy can become your philosophy, and this book will show you how to make that happen.

Where to start

1. Begin by embracing the Mackenbach philosophy. Say out loud to yourself, "I am responsible for the success of each and every one of my relationships." Print these words on a card and tape it on the wall of your office, your kitchen, your bathroom. Carry it in your wallet. Read, think, and say these words to yourself over and over again. Embed them in your mind.
2. Make it easy for people to be nice to you. Greet them with a friendly smile. Be patient with their inadequacies and understanding of their problems. If you brighten their day, they will brighten yours.
3. If you're engaged in ongoing conflict with someone with whom you have a close personal relationship (a family member, a friend, a partner or colleague), pay close atten-

tion to how you're playing out the dance. Note where your actions are reinforcing the patterns of chronic negative behavior that seem to define the relationship.

My associate and I were locked in a pattern of "push-withdraw-push-withdraw." Occasionally a mini-pattern would emerge—an abrupt two-step within the waltz where I would push, she would lash out at me, I would defend myself, she would withdraw—and then we'd be right back in the old familiar rhythms. I could have interrupted the cycle at some point if, instead of pushing, I had acted differently. But at the time it didn't occur to me, and if it had, I wouldn't have known what to do. So I just went on being the same old me, only more so.

Taking responsibility is the first step in knowing what to do. The next step is to understand exactly what conflict is and where it comes from. Knowledge is power, and the more you know about the essence and origins of conflict, the more tools for its management you'll have at your disposal.

2

The Nature of Conflict

Recently I was asked to speak at an organization's annual "education day" retreat. As I was discussing topics with the program committee, I suggested it might be worthwhile to do a workshop on conflict management. "Oh, no, not conflict" someone exclaimed. "That's much too negative."

The very idea of conflict upsets people. At one time, I thought only timid people avoid confrontation—that more assertive people are able to manage it without getting upset, and aggressors actively seek it out because they think conflict is fun. But we've conducted some informal studies over the years and discovered that almost everyone hates conflict, even hard-nosed, seemingly belligerent individuals who never seem to shy away from a fight.

What words come to your mind when you hear the word "conflict"? Common responses from our workshop attendees have been:

disagreement	clash	tension
quarrel	hostility	pain
strife	war	anxiety
misunderstanding	agony	argument
anger	battle	dispute

These words are all negative, which illustrates the fact that most people see conflict in negative terms, something to be avoided whenever possible. Here is how a businessman who attended one of our workshops explained it: "As long as I'm the good guy, I'm okay. But the minute I get attacked, I can feel myself freeze. It doesn't seem to matter whether the issues are big or little. My muscles get tight, and my head pounds so hard that I can barely hear myself talk. It's like I turn to stone. I know I'm able to hide what I'm feeling inside, but people see me shut down, and that's not good."

Another attendee put it this way. "I can't stand it when people get emotional. When they get angry and shout or break down and cry, I never know what to do. So I just lay down the law and walk out." She thought for a moment and then added, "I always end up with a stomachache."

Conflict is emotional

Conflict *is* emotional. That's why dealing with it is so difficult. If the emotions weren't involved, conflict would be nothing more than problem solving. Eavesdrop for a moment on a conversation between Bill and Dan.

Bill: *Why did you change the procedure without telling me?*

Dan: *I thought it would improve the situation.*

Bill: *You didn't answer my question.*

Dan: *My intentions were good because I felt this would help. I didn't think it would create a problem and I thought I should take some initiative.*

Bill: *We have procedures here that must be followed. You can't run off and do whatever you please. Your good intentions have just confused everything. You know what the procedures are, don't you?*

Dan: *Yes, but . . .*

Bill: *No buts. You must present any changes you're considering to me. No exceptions.*

Dan: *Okay.*

This conversation appears to be about the logical consequences of not following procedures. If we were to ask Bill, he would say it's a very simple matter. You either follow the rules or you don't, and if you don't you get in trouble. Perfectly logical, right?

Right. The *problem* is with the procedures set forth by the company and whether or not they're being followed (or need to be changed). Solving the problem is a thinking process. The *conflict* is over feelings and each man's perceptions of his own power. Bill feels ignored when Dan doesn't check with him before taking initiative on his watch. Although he would never admit it, he feels powerless as a manager when he's not consulted. His feelings when he's chastised by his own boss go beyond embarrassment. He's humiliated by Dan's actions.

On the other hand, Dan wants to feel in control of his own job. He was proud of the initiative he took. But now his feelings of pride have degenerated into helplessness. He feels muzzled. Is he likely to put forth an idea ever again? Probably not.

No matter what management theory is currently in vogue, "emotion" seems to remain a dirty word in most organizations. Thinking is rational, decisions are made logically, and actions are always strategic. Or so they say. The truth is that emotions are always a key factor in interpersonal relationships, and if you deny their presence, you'll miss every opportunity to successfully manage the conflicts in your life.

Definition of Conflict

Every researcher who has ever studied conflict has developed his or her own definition. Most of these definitions are filled with five-syllable words and are difficult to translate into understandable, usable terms. A simpler definition—one that works well for our purposes—is found in *Webster's New Collegiate Dictionary*: "the struggle resulting from incompatible or opposing interests, wants, needs, or drives." A teenager's need to be independent clashes with a parent's desire to keep the kid from getting into trouble. A manager's business goal of achieving higher results with fewer resources (which means overtime) collides with the employee's personal goal of spending more time with her children. A company must cut costs in order to stay profitable; yet the employees aren't about to give up their health benefits.

In each of these cases, the interests or needs of one party are opposed by the interests or needs of the other party. As the parties struggle to achieve their own goals, conflict ensues and often escalates as they dig their heels in and defend their own positions.

Unless Bill and Dan learn new skills, their conflict will persist. Bill will continue to feed his desire to control by forcefully exerting his authority and demanding blind obedience from the members of his group, who in turn will resist him by becoming more and more passive. Dejected and morose, Dan will come to work, do his job, and go home at the appointed time, never again to feel the excitement and satisfaction of being a full contributor. And since it's always the other guy's fault, each will blame the other for making his own job that much harder.

There's a better way

If conflict is the struggle that results from incompatible or opposing interests, wants, needs, or drives, then it's pretty obvious that we're going to encounter it everywhere. I don't know anyone in the world whose interests, wants, needs, and drives are exactly the same as mine (and I can't imagine you do either), because our temperaments, backgrounds, education, life experiences, occupations, and lifestyles will never all be the same. So sooner or later we're going to find ourselves in conflict with somebody else. It's part of the natural order, and since all things natural contain both positive and negative forces, we need now to look at the constructive side of conflict. A new list of more positive words to describe "conflict" might contain:

opportunity	challenge	advancement
progress	understanding	growth
creation	daring	healing
excitement	satisfaction	reality
energy	boldness	adventure

The Chinese character for conflict is made up of two symbols—one signifying danger, the other opportunity. Social scientists have theorized that no significant social change can take place without the struggle that occurs when interests/needs collide. If people were happy with the status quo, there would be no need for change, and everyone would remain blissfully content with things "just like they've always been." It's only when there's unrest that opportunities for improvement occur.

Conflict is normal

Managing conflict successfully doesn't mean "getting back to normal." There is no "normal," if by normal we mean returning to the status quo. Mom doesn't like the loud, obnoxious, addicted-to-bathroom-humor teenager her child has become. She wants her little boy back. But the little boy has become a big boy, and with that growth, a new and different family structure has emerged, one that demands new and different relationships. The *opportunity* is there to create stronger family ties that include honor, trust, and mutual respect—a far cry from the parent/child patterns of the past, but just as satisfying and just as loving.

For Bill, "getting back to normal" means that Dan will remember to ask permission if he wants to try something new. But this isn't really normal, it's just the "current situation," one that is likely to explode all over again the next time someone in the group strikes out on his own. The *opportunity* is there to unite the group in a spirit of teamwork and initiative, so everyone feels involved and Bill can become a cheerleader, instead of a disciplinarian.

When I was in conflict with my colleague, I was determined that she would be enthusiastic, cooperative, and uncritical—exactly like she had been before we began to argue. I wanted to "get back to normal," so the business wouldn't suffer. The *opportunity* was there for us to recognize how the growth of the business was demanding changes in our relationship, and to view the situation as a force for positive action instead of an unavoidable disaster. In other words, the opportunity was there to create a new "normal."

My interests, wants, needs, and drives are normal. So are yours. It's normal that if we live, or play, or work together, we will find ourselves in disagreement at least some of the time. The state of conflict is a normal state; we can't eliminate it from our lives, nor should we try. It's part of the natural order.

Next steps

1. Remember that opposition to your getting what you want can occur at any time; lashing out in anger will only make matters worse, while succumbing to it will turn you into a victim. As part of the natural order, interpersonal conflict has always been, and will always be, with us. Without it our lives would become stagnant.
2. Recognize and accept the presence of strong emotions in every conflict situation, both those of your conflict partner and your own. **Do not deny these emotions.** In future chapters, I'll show you how to handle them.
3. Think of conflict in constructive terms. Although it may seem scary, reframe it as an opportunity to develop into a more positive, confident, and influential human being. Learning to meet and master the challenge of interpersonal conflict can be one of life's great adventures.

3

What Are We Fighting About?

If you and I live or work together, conflicts between us are inevitable. My interests/needs will sooner or later collide with yours; our emotions will be engaged, and the battle will be on. What will we fight over? For the most part, we'll fight over substance and we'll fight over relationships.

Fighting over substance

Substance issues are content-oriented, objective issues over where to go, what to do, what decisions to make, how to spend the money, what action to take, etc. A substance issue is really a problem to be solved. It can be written down, studied, and argued over, the final outcome determined by cool-headed analysis and planning. With careful deliberation, answers to even the most difficult content-oriented questions can be found, thereby releasing us to go cheerfully about our business. Even when emotions enter the picture and turn the problem into a conflict, the basic issue is still one of substance or content. Here are some examples.

- Two managers have been charged with drafting a marketing plan for the company's growth. Sarah favors expanding into new territories, increasing the number of representatives in each territory, and going after new markets. Ken thinks these ideas are too ambitious; for him, the way to grow is to get more dollars from existing customers. To do this, he wants to develop new products and increase the size of the entertainment budget. Although both Sarah and Ken feel they are right and argue intensely the merits of their case, this is essentially a fight over substance—how to allocate the company's resources to provide the greatest growth.

- A couple has decided to buy a house but can't agree yet on location or initial condition of their new home. He wants to live in an older neighborhood and is excited about buying a fixer-upper and renovating it to their own specifications. She is a working mother and the very thought of a do-it-yourself project exhausts her. She wants a brand new house in a development full of young families with lots of kids. He's dying to be a handyman; she wants no part of it.

- Jeff has received an offer for the position he feels is the culmination of his entire career. However, taking the new job will mean a relocation from Albany to Phoenix. Jeff's wife, Mara, has just started her own business, and their son and daughter are enrolled in a fine private school where they are both well liked and academically successful. In addition, Jeff's widowed mother lives three blocks from their suburban home, where she is able to be part of the family and yet retain her independence. Each party in this scenario has a whole sackful of interests/needs that are likely to conflict with Jeff's strong need to succeed in his career.

Although in each of these cases the emotions of the parties can and probably will influence the final outcome, the eventual resolution of each conflict will require clear thinking and a thorough weighing of the pros and cons. They are all substance-based but not always recognized or managed as such.

Fighting over relationships

Relationship issues are all about who we are in *relation* to each other. What do you mean to me? What do I mean to you? How important are you in my life (and I in yours)? What power do we have over each other and how comfortable am I with that? Do we speak individually or as one? The closer our relationship, the more we are likely to fight over it. And sometimes substance and relationship are hard to separate.

In Chapter 1, Brenda's conflict with Jane is a good example of a content cum relationship issue. Jane wasn't thinking about her relationship with Brenda when she asked for a favor. She needed to get something in the mail, and for her the *substance* of the issue was results-oriented: who would type the document. Brenda's concern, however, was for the *relationship*. She wanted Jane to be sensitive to her need to close the books, just as she was sensitive to Jane's need to meet her deadline. Brenda wanted an *equal* relationship built on mutual consideration and respect.

Let's revisit Sarah and Ken and revise their conflict over the planning project into one not just of substance but of relationships. Let's say Ken has worked for the company longer than Sarah. In fact, he's been the president's right-hand man for as long as he can remember. Now it looks to him like Sarah is becoming the favored one. She and the president have long talks after work; they seem to agree on almost everything, and they laugh a lot together, as if they were sharing secrets. Ken is terrified that he's losing ground and will soon be shunted aside and forgotten. His fight over the allocation of resources has become a fight over territory—his position as the star performer, and hence his relationship with the president.

Sarah, on the other hand, just wants to be on equal footing with Ken. She knows they'll be working together for a long time; their relationship is as important to her as the plan itself, and she wants that recognition of parity from Ken. The fact that he seems to regard her as a threat upsets Sarah, and she's vowed not to let him diminish her contribution. In this new scenario, the conflict is about far more than just a marketing plan; it's about vital relationships between, and among, Sarah, Ken, and the company president.

What else is the fight over?

Substance and relationship issues are inherent in every conflict interaction, especially if the relationships are close ones. In addition, we need to look at some of the external causes of conflict, those elements that trigger the fight and in many instances become its content.

Competition for limited resources. The pie never seems to be quite big enough. There's only so much money to spend. Who gets it? Which projects get funded and which fall by the wayside? Who gets the office with the view of the lake?

Turf battles and power struggles are illustrations of competition for perceived limited resources. Sibling rivalry is nothing more than kids fighting over what they *perceive* as limited parental love. Somehow they don't feel there's enough to go around. Ken is fighting for his "place" at the side of the company's president as if there were only room for one person. In fact, there are probably times that the president feels like a parent caught up in the endless squabbles of recalcitrant teenagers. Whenever resources appear to be limited, people will fight over them. Good negotiators make sure there's something for everyone in the final agreement, that each party feels like a winner, and that no one is completely left out.

Unclear roles and responsibilities. I once watched a business owner interview and hire a "marketer." In the interviews, all the discussion was about marketing. The individual who was hired had a degree in marketing. The position carried the title "Marketing Specialist." Unfortunately for everyone, the *real* job was in sales, but nobody said anything about sales, because to the business owner, "sales" was a dirty word. Six miserable months later, the marketer was gone because he didn't sell anything. Anger and bitterness all around.

It's easy for managers to assume that everyone in the group understands everyone else's roles, but this is often not the case. Leslie had been working congenially with five other researchers in a laboratory when she was promoted to lab manager, her very first supervisory position. The only problem was that no one told the researchers that Leslie had become their manager, and no one advised Leslie on how to handle this difficult transition. Not surprisingly, when Leslie tried to manage, everyone got mad. When one of the researchers (who had been a good friend) got married, Leslie was the only person in the lab who didn't get invited to the wedding. Loss of friendship and loss of productivity—everyone lost on this one.

One of the most common causes of conflict in the workplace is unclear roles and responsibilities. When you're trying to discover the cause of an office conflict, you might want to begin by asking people to write down their responsibilities as they *perceive* them, along with the tasks they actually perform every day. Chart their responses in a group meeting and compare each individual's perceptions with those of the group as a whole. You and everyone in the office are likely to be surprised.

Change. Not long ago, I asked a group how many people were presently experiencing significant change in their lives. Every hand went up. We are in the midst of great societal change. Nothing seems stable; governments, businesses and corporations, entire industries, offices, school systems, families—everywhere the old cultures are disappearing and, until new cultures are formed, chaos reigns. This is a natural breeding ground for conflict, particularly when people feel their share of the pie is shrinking right before their eyes. Woodrow Wilson said, "If you want to make enemies, try to change something."

Differing expectations. In *My Fair Lady,* Henry Higgins sings plaintively, "Why can't a woman be like ME?" It's so easy to see the world only through our own eyes. Everyone should think like we think, do like we do, look like we look, talk like we talk, feel like we feel . . . and the list goes on and on. If I *want* you to be like me, and you're not, I'll be disappointed. If I *expect* you to be like me, and you're not, I'll be angry and frustrated. And if I expect you to be like me and then *treat* you according to that expectation, we will be in conflict. My interest in neatness turns into my expectation that you will be neat. Then when you continually track up my clean floor with your muddy boots and don't even say you're sorry, you've got trouble, buster.

So-called personality clashes are a result of differing expectations of how the parties *should* behave. So are lack of cooperation and noncompliance with official rules and policies. So are racial and cultural differences that pit us against each other because, "You're different; you're not like me." Insisting that someone change in order to live up to your expectations is futile. Remember, you can't change the other guy; the responsibility to change the patterns that define the relationship is yours.

Misunderstandings. An acquaintance once graciously lent me a book from his prized library with the stipulation that I would return it just as soon as I had read it. Well, this was a very long book, and as my usual procedure was to read a few pages every evening before falling asleep, the book stayed on my nightstand table for some time. Two weeks or so later, I received an abrupt call from the owner. "Where is my book," he commanded. "I want it back." I immediately returned his book, unread.

Another time, an associate and I were on a late flight into

Cleveland after a grueling four-day workshop schedule. As we parted at the airport, I said, "Take your time coming in tomorrow morning." When she showed up at 10:30 AM, my first comment was, unfortunately, "Where have you been?" Her response came immediately. "Carolyn, we all know that for you, 'take your time coming in' means no later than 8:30, but that really doesn't work for the rest of us. Next time, I guess we need to be a little more specific about how long I can sleep in."

When my mental picture of a situation isn't quite the same as your mental picture of the same situation, we have a misunderstanding. A mistake often happens because of mismatched pictures. Usually it's no big deal, and if that's the case, let it go. We spend too much of our time trying to figure out *who* to blame, when it's better to just chalk the mistake up to a misunderstanding and move on. (Just be sure when you borrow something, you find out exactly when the lender wants it back.)

Action Steps

1. Examine an interpersonal conflict in your life and see if it's basically about substance. Or does the state of the relationship play a big part? Are you able to separate the two issues, or do they seem inextricably intertwined?
2. Try to determine the external conditions or situations that have triggered your conflict. Is it caused, wholly or in part, by competition, unclear roles, change, differing expectations, rash assumptions? Or did it start from a plain old misunderstanding? Do you see other causes that haven't been mentioned here?

4

Know Yourself

How do you respond to conflict? When you and your conflict partner are locked in battle, nose to nose, what do you usually say? What do you usually do? Social scientists have identified five fairly common responses to conflict: denial, avoidance, accommodation, force, and negotiation. As part of your general conflict management repertoire, these responses can all be useful. However, repeated, habitual use of any one response, whether it works or not, will turn it into a less flexible conflict *style*, which will reduce your overall effectiveness.

The five conflict styles

Denial. To deny a problem is to pretend it doesn't exist. Perhaps you're afraid of facing up to it. Or perhaps you just aren't interested, as was the case with the executive director of a charitable organization I once worked with. Concerned about the lack of diversity in its staff, the board asked for a review of the organization's hiring practices. The executive director refused. "We have an equal employment policy," he stated, "and there is no problem here." As a matter of fact, there *was* a problem in the organization, and by denying it the director was actually contributing to it.

Denial can feel good. It seems to ease the pressure; if you refuse to recognize the problem, there's nothing to worry about and you won't have to take any action. But this is false complacency, because, whatever your reasons, your denial of the problem won't make it go away. In fact, it will probably make your conflict partner crazy—a surefire way to escalate the conflict. In personal relationships, this can be especially frustrating.

He: *What's the matter, honey?*
She: *Nothing.*
He: *Well, you sure seem upset about something.*
She: *I'm telling you, nothing's the matter.*
He: *You haven't said two words all evening. I can tell something's bothering you.*
She: *Nothing's bothering me. I don't want to talk about it.*
He: *Talk about what?*
She: *Nothing.*

Avoidance. Have you ever noticed that when you get the job they call you on the telephone, but when you don't get the job they send you a letter? Some people will go to almost any length to avoid confrontation; they want to protect themselves (and often their partners) from unpleasantness and strife. Tom's boss knew that Tom wasn't going to get the promotion he wanted so badly; the decision had been made to bring in new blood from outside the firm. Deep down, Tom's boss knew that to be fair he should tell Tom of his decision. But because he feared the confrontation, he told himself he didn't want to hurt Tom and kept silent. When Tom heard the news from someone else, he felt betrayed, and his anguish so affected morale in the office that the new person didn't have a chance.

As a short-term tactic, avoidance can be effective, especially if the issue isn't a particularly important one. Some issues just aren't worth the trouble, and some disagreements will fade away on their own. But you'll make matters worse if you look the other way and what's not important to *you* turns out to be very important to someone else. In the long run, avoidance, like denial, does nothing to ease the conflict and will only prolong a difficult situation.

Accommodation. Accommodators will yield on almost every issue because they believe peace and harmony are worth whatever price is demanded. They just can't say no. John is a people pleaser and wants everyone to be happy, even at his own expense. For him the path of least resistance is to give in. As a result, people in his close circle (parents, children, wife, ex-wife, boss, and co-workers) tend to take advantage of him, often calling at the last minute with requests that, at least on their agendas, seem urgent. In most cases, however, these are trivial things that could wait a day or even longer. Or they're the result of someone else's incompetence or lack of planning—not his responsibility. Usually John drops what he's doing and responds. "It's okay," he says over and over. "I don't mind. . . really I don't."

Don't be misled. Doing nice things for the people we like or love isn't a bad thing; kindness and accommodation are an integral part of any healthy relationship and give all of us pleasure. But John's habitual acquiescence has established patterns that will be extremely difficult to break. If he keeps on giving in, the world will keep on taking advantage of him.

Force. Forcers use the power of their position or their personality to control. They make decisions quickly and let you know in no uncertain terms that they are *never* wrong. Sometimes forcers are shouters and sometimes they are strong, silent types. Either way, they rule by intimidation, and people back down because they don't feel strong enough, or don't know how, to fight back.

Often power is inherent in a position of status or hierarchy, and people respond to the *perception* of force, even if it doesn't actually exist. If you're my "superior," I may feel that you hold my destiny in the palm of your hand. Acting on that assumption, I will obey you or agree with you (even if I think you're wrong), because I'm convinced that if I don't, you'll fire me . . . demote me . . . flunk me . . . embarrass me . . . do something to me that will cause me harm. In other cases, forcers *intentionally* use their position to control. "Why do you have to do this? Because I'm your mother and I said so, that's why."

There are times when it's appropriate to make use of power to get things done. The midst of a crisis isn't the time or the place for consensus building; when the building's burning, it's foolish to waste time trying to agree on who jumps out which window. Corporate turn-around artists are called in to rescue failing organizations and must make quick decisions about who stays, who goes, and how the company will be run in the immediate future. In these situations, action, not talk, is needed and someone must be in charge. However, the chronic use of force destroys teamwork and inhibits group participation, and over time it will exacerbate the very conflict it's meant to control.

Negotiation. To negotiate is to reach a settlement by conference, discussion, or compromise. At its best, negotiation doesn't end until both parties feel they're winners, and when your conflict partner is also a partner in life or business, a mutually beneficial, negotiated settlement is a worthy goal.

Negotiation is neither quick nor easy, and there are times when it becomes an impractical choice (as in the cases of the burning building and the failing organization). It also takes skill and diplomacy. Additionally, we tend to view negotiation as a purely transactional matter, as when we're negotiating a labor contract, a salary increase, or a car deal. In *interpersonal* conflict, the tendency is to fall back on one of the other four responses, precisely because it *is* quicker and easier to do so. But even though you want to grind the other person into the ground and destroy him forever (this is the forcer route), a satisfying, long-lasting settlement depends upon your providing the other side with a win, too.

It's a matter of balance

When I was growing up, I was continually criticized for the very characteristics that make me who I am. "You're too impatient, Carolyn," I was told by the adults around me. "You move too fast, you're too decisive, you're too eager, *you're too smart for your own good."* Hearing this year in and year out, I came to believe that these characteristics were bad and that I had to get rid of them and develop all new qualities—that the person I *should* be was the exact opposite of the person I already was. This denial of self, even though it's based on misinformation, is incredibly damaging to the human spirit.

My personal characteristics were not inherently bad, even though as a child and young adult I believed this to be true. In reality, they were the very characteristics that made me strong and eventually allowed me to build a successful business. What I needed to do was *balance* them with other, seemingly contradictory, qualities that didn't come quite as naturally to me. At VOICE-PRO, we call this model *The Balanced Communicator*™

Imagine yourself standing at the center of a seesaw. On one side of the board are the "soft" people-oriented qualities: pleasantness, flexibility, patience, tact, and open-minded-ness. On the other side are the balancing "stronger" qualities: firmness, consistency, action, directness, and decisiveness. In order to keep your balance, you must put pressure first on your left foot and then on your right. By equalizing the pressure, you'll be able to keep from sliding too far to one side or the other. Effective communicators are always performing a juggling act. First the board tilts one way, and to balance it we become stronger; then it tilts the other way, and we must let our softer side take over.

Not either/or but both/and

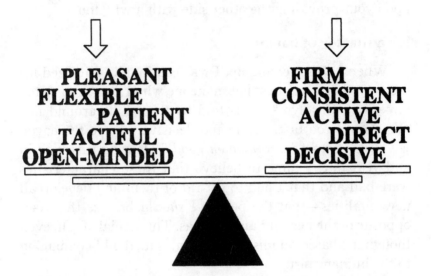

On the left side of the seesaw are the "soft" qualities, often associated with the people, or relationship, side of the conflict. On the right, are the "strong" qualities, which are identified with problem solving (the substance side of the conflict). While some people are more naturally inclined toward the left and others to the right, there is no either/or about it. The "either/or" syndrome is one of the great fallacies of our society—a simplistic approach that eliminates options and positive thinking. We must possess—or develop if we don't have them—qualities on both sides of the board. My inherent characteristics, the ones for which I was criticized, are on the right; and instead of being ashamed of them, I now celebrate them. I also make sure that I continue to cultivate the qualities of pleasantness, flexibility, patience, tact, and open-mindedness, so that my overall behavior remains in balance and my relationships don't suffer because I have a one-sided personality.

Pleasant yet firm. I once worked with a choir director who everyone said was "too nice." Like John, the accommodator, Lawrence was always being taken advantage of by the members of the choir. We were chronically late to rehearsal, sang the wrong notes, and talked while other singers were working—truly an undisciplined lot. When Lawrence heard the complaints about his being "too nice," he (like me) misinterpreted it to mean that "nice" was bad. So periodically he would storm into rehearsal, slam his music down on the stand, and harshly berate us for being poor musicians. After a while, because this was so foreign to his nature (and didn't work anyway), he would revert to his old, pleasant self, at which point we went right back to our unprofessional behavior, and the dance began anew.

Being "too nice" isn't possible; being pleasant without having a corresponding firmness of resolve is very possible. Lawrence didn't need to yell at us. He needed to establish clear and fair rules of behavior for the choir, including being on time, prepared, and courteous of others. Then he needed to enforce those rules firmly, even if it meant expelling singers who didn't comply. And he could do all of this without giving up the pleasant manner that was so much a part of him. "Nice" wasn't the problem; not being firm was very much the problem.

Flexible yet consistent. As we've discussed so far, in order to manage conflict, you must, first, take responsibility for improving the relationship with your conflict partner; second, change the patterns by adjusting your own behavior; and third, develop a repertoire of conflict responses instead of adhering to one particular style. These actions all require flexibility—the ability and willingness to respond quickly to changing circumstances. If a door closes, another door will open. If one idea doesn't work, try another.

Balancing the willingness to bend is the quality of consistency, or constancy of purpose. If you've ever worked with someone whose behavior was so unpredictable that you didn't know from moment to moment how she would respond, you know how important the quality of consistency is. A mistake made yesterday was shrugged off; a similar mistake today becomes grounds for execution. You never know where you stand with a person whose behavior is inconsistent. Parents lament the volatile behavior of their teenagers, but at least that behavior can be explained away as overactive hormones. In adults, for whom there is no such excuse, lack of consistency can ruin a relationship. At its worst it can poison an entire organization, especially if the inconsistent person plays a senior role.

Patient yet active. The impatience I've been criticized for my whole life is in reality a penchant for action. "When in doubt, do something," is my motto. If there's a problem, fix it—if there's a decision to be made, make it—if there's work to be done, get on with it. This penchant for action can be a huge advantage, especially in situations where decisions need to be made and the work needs to get done. But it's also necessary for me, and others like me, to understand the benefits of timing and to learn when to push and when to hold back.

Improving the relationships in our lives takes time. We must keep reminding ourselves that our own patterns won't change overnight and our conflict partners will adjust only gradually, and perhaps reluctantly, to the new dance. This is not an instantaneous happening, it's a process that takes place over a long period of time, and sometimes we just have to wait. With patience, our action orientation is a plus; without it, we're just bulldozers.

Tactful yet direct. The seesaw can swing widely between tact and directness. Being honest about your thoughts and feelings is a wonderful quality. People know where they stand with you when you're direct with them. When they ask a question, you give them an answer. If you can help them, you do it; if you can't help them, you say so. At the same time, directness needs to be accompanied by tact, otherwise your candor will deteriorate into rudeness. Treat other people with respect, no matter how angry and resentful you feel. Acknowledge their point of view, avoid inflam-

matory words, and, above all, don't blame or become judgmental. Through the skilled use of diplomacy, you'll be able
to get your own interests/needs met without trampling on
the interests/needs of your conflict partner.

John, the accommodator, on the other hand, overdoes
tact. He says whatever he thinks the other person wants to
hear. He apologizes over things that aren't his fault so the
other person's feelings won't be hurt. He takes no initiative
because he's always waiting to see where the discussion goes
before he agrees or disagrees (and he almost always agrees).
At times, to his dismay, he's even suspected of being devious,
since his lack of directness leaves his companions confused
about his motives.

Open-minded yet decisive. There are vast differences in
the speed with which individuals make decisions. Some folks
decide quickly, based on their gut reactions, and justify their
decisions later; others gather and analyze all the relevant data,
then make informed choices in a logical, rational manner. The
second way takes longer. Quick decision makers need to be
open to new possibilities and willing to listen to others' ideas
and opinions *before* they jump to their conclusions.
Thoughtful decision makers need to realize that all decisions
are made on the basis of insufficient data, and that eventually
they must grab the bull by the horns and just . . . decide.

Next step

Take the Proverbs test. A proverb is a brief, popular saying that contains a general truth. Each of the proverbs illustrates a conflict resolution philosophy. Think of a specific
conflict in your life and check the proverbs that best
describe your responses in that situation. Then ask yourself,
is this how I've responded to other conflicts I've experienced? Is this typical behavior for me? Remember, each of
these proverbs has a grain of truth in it, so there are no
wrong answers. In this exercise, you're looking for patterns,
and you're looking for ways to know yourself better.

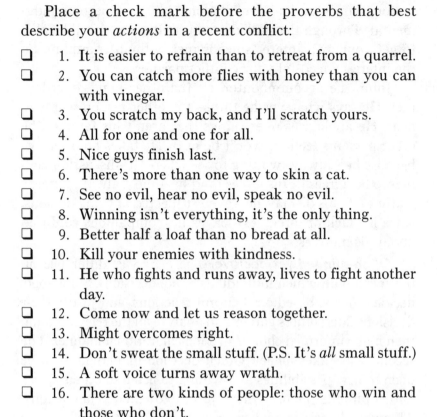

Place a check mark before the proverbs that best describe your *actions* in a recent conflict:

- ❑   1. It is easier to refrain than to retreat from a quarrel.
- ❑   2. You can catch more flies with honey than you can with vinegar.
- ❑   3. You scratch my back, and I'll scratch yours.
- ❑   4. All for one and one for all.
- ❑   5. Nice guys finish last.
- ❑   6. There's more than one way to skin a cat.
- ❑   7. See no evil, hear no evil, speak no evil.
- ❑   8. Winning isn't everything, it's the only thing.
- ❑   9. Better half a loaf than no bread at all.
- ❑ 10. Kill your enemies with kindness.
- ❑ 11. He who fights and runs away, lives to fight another day.
- ❑ 12. Come now and let us reason together.
- ❑ 13. Might overcomes right.
- ❑ 14. Don't sweat the small stuff. (P.S. It's *all* small stuff.)
- ❑ 15. A soft voice turns away wrath.
- ❑ 16. There are two kinds of people: those who win and those who don't.
- ❑ 17. Pretty is as pretty does.

Be honest with yourself. Did you answer the way you think you *should* have acted, or did you answer the way you really behaved? If you checked 1, 7, 11, and 14, your tendency is to deny or avoid the unpleasantness of conflict. Numbers 2, 10, 15, and 17, indicate accommodation as a conflict style; and 5, 8, 13, and 16 indicate your propensity to use power to control. The negotiation style is denoted by numbers 3, 4, 6, 9, and 12. A mixture of responses suggests that you aren't locked in one particular style and use a variety of responses depending on the situation.

You might want to give yourself a reality check by asking a friend, a spouse, or a trusted colleague to take the test on your behalf. We're often amazed to find that other people have entirely different perceptions of us than we have of ourselves. This can be a bit hard on the ego, but it's a valuable exercise in itself.

Denial, avoidance, and accommodation lie to the extreme left of the board on our *Balanced Communicator*™ seesaw, while force falls on the far right. If you're a good negotiator, you're nicely balanced in the middle most of the time.

I hope by this time you have a good sense of how you respond to conflict. Your awareness is a prerequisite for what lies ahead: the six steps that will enable you to shift the dance from conflict to compatibility. As I said, it's often helpful to ask someone close to you (with whom you're *not* fighting) to go through the Proverbs test with you and see if his assessment is the same as yours. But you may be impatient (on the right side of the seesaw board) and are thinking that we've *talked* about conflict long enough, and now it's time to *do* something. If that's the case, read on.

5

The Six Steps to Compatibility

Compatibility—the state of existing together in harmony—is what we want for ourselves and our conflict partners. At work, I want to be treated with respect. I want my ideas considered in the collegial spirit in which I offer them and my efforts noticed and acknowledged. I don't need to be agreed with all the time; but I always want to be heard. And because I'm responsible for the success of my relationships, it becomes my obligation to return in kind the behavior I desire from others. At home it's no different. I want to create an environment where every individual is a *valued* member of the family, cherished for who we are as well as what we can contribute.

The compatible organization

All compatible organizations, whether they're offices, factories, homes, or schools, have certain commonalities. Let's look at what goes on at AccuTech Industries, a mid-size manufacturer of precision machine tools. At AccuTech, there is a well-defined structure that everybody understands and accepts. AccuTech's managers spend a lot of time making sure that both goals and roles are clear. Continual discussions revolve around the framework of the structure and how to make it better, but seldom around the need for the structure itself. The structure is a flexible one that can adapt quickly to both inside and outside influences. AccuTech is a living, evolving organism, and everyone is accordingly responsive.

From the CEO's office to the plant floor during the night shift, AccuTech employees treat each other with courtesy and respect. Mistakes and misunderstandings are viewed as "learning by experience" and opportunities to make things better. Even when people are angry and frustrated, they make it clear that it's the *events* that are the problem, not the people involved. They then attack the *problem*, not the people. There is also a high respect for individualism. The "you're different from me, therefore we won't be able to get along" syndrome doesn't exist at AccuTech. Talents are celebrated for the value they bring to the table, allowance is made for contrasting work styles, and initiative is appreciated and rewarded, not perceived as threatening.

Open, honest discussion without fear is a fundamental component of AccuTech's culture. Differences of opinion are encouraged, and debates are often heated, with people arguing passionately for what they believe in. Everyone is trained to respond quickly and quietly to personal grievances, so they are dealt with by the involved parties themselves, and negative groundswell is never allowed to infect the whole group. The result is that people look forward to coming to work. They are productive, they feel needed and fulfilled, and they have fun. And they are extremely protective of their very special culture, with each and every individual committed to upholding and preserving it.

We all want to live and work in compatible organizations, but they don't happen by themselves. Every organization is a group of individuals who are either in a state of conflict or a state of compatibility with other individuals. The organization doesn't decide it's going to be compatible, the people within the organization—each and every one—make that choice.

The balance of this book will provide you with a step-by-step method for handling yourself well whenever you find yourself locking horns with your conflict partner, so that, in the heat of the moment, you'll act in ways that will transform the dance and move the two of you out of conflict and into the state of compatibility. Here is an overview of this six-step process, which starts with understanding not just the nature of *any* conflict but the nature of *your* conflict.

The Six Steps

Step 1: Analyze your conflict. It's difficult to resolve a conflict when you don't really understand it. You think you're fighting about one thing when in reality the issue is something entirely different. As you learn the ways to define and analyze your conflict, you'll gain insights into the motives for your own behavior, as well as those of your conflict partner, and be better able to handle the sticky moments that lie ahead.

Step 2: Determine your goals and priorities. In your heart of hearts, you may want to beat the other person into submission, forcing him to admit that you were right all along. This may make you feel good in the short run, but in the long run it isn't likely to get you what you really want. You need to think ahead, determine your desired outcome, and set your priorities. What will the picture be like when your conflict is successfully resolved? What do you need to accomplish in order to make that picture happen?

Step 3: Keep your cool; keep your power. In the Old West, it was socially acceptable to shoot someone as long as he fired first. Aggression was met by aggression, a deadly example of the "push/push back" phenomenon. If people hurt us, the natural response is to want to give them a shove right back. But the more we "shoot back," the more likely the conflict is to escalate. The tactics to be described in Step 3 will help you remain calm under pressure and maintain your poise when others are losing theirs.

Step 4: Listen until you understand. Listening means fully understanding the message from your *conflict partner's* point of view and accepting the fact that to her that point of view is valid. Listening is more than just being silent until it's your turn to talk; it demands your active participation during the entire interaction. And while it's recognized as a key component in the success of every personal interaction, listening may be the most difficult of all the communication skills to master. It's hard to be a good listener.

Step 5: Talk from your point of view. When you take the usual route and view conflict as the other guy's fault, it becomes incredibly easy to blame and criticize. This is *not* the way to manage conflicts in a fair and equitable way. Actually, it's not the way to manage conflicts at all. You'll eliminate the need for your antagonist to become defensive if you talk about how *you* feel and what *you* intend to do. The tactics described in Step 5 will help you do this.

Step 6: Move to problem solving. Earlier I said that a conflict with the emotion removed becomes a problem to be solved. Steps 4 and 5 deal directly with the emotional elements of conflict. Step 6 shows you how to deal with the conflict's substance and find a way together to move forward with everyone feeling like a winner.

Take it step by step

As part of a sales training exercise, a friend of mine was asked to select a target customer on which to practice. His assignment was to proceed, step by step, through the selling cycle; the goal was to master the process, not necessarily to make the sale. My friend chose a company where he had no past history, so the emotional stakes for him were low. The company also had need of the services he offered, so the possibilities for success were relatively high. In short, his target provided him with a situation where he had a reasonably good chance for success.

As part of your first attempt at implementation of the six

steps, I suggest you do the same. Choose a conflict where you're experiencing only a moderate level of emotional intensity. (If you're already at the emotional breaking point, you might want to practice on a different conflict.) Your choice should be one where you and your conflict partner have built up a reservoir of trust, so you're not building the relationship from scratch. In other words, start with a small conflict. You'll be able to proceed to larger, more difficult ones as your skills increase.

Consider this a practice exercise and work through each step in its entirety; the process needs to be completed in the order I've laid out here. As with my friend who was learning the selling cycle, you'll do better if you understand the process, so don't jump around—at least not at first. Later, when you've become proficient, you'll know instinctively when to talk and when to listen, and you'll automatically define and redefine the conflict whenever necessary. To help you, a graphic model of the six steps appears in the appendix at the end of the book. "Patience," I say to all you action-oriented individuals in the meantime. "On this first pass, take it in order."

Things may get worse before they get better

In a perfect world, you would breeze through the six steps, at which point your partner would say, "Wow, you're absolutely right and I'm absolutely wrong. As of this very moment my wicked ways are mended, and I thank you from the bottom of my heart for telling me how mean I've been to you." Then the two of you would live happily ever after. Of course, this isn't a perfect world, and not many people will thank you for upsetting the status quo.

According to the Encyclopedia Britannica, *homeostasis* is "a term that refers to the ability of a living organism to maintain a stable set of conditions inside its body." For example, if you go outside on a hot day, your homeostatic reflexes help you maintain a stable internal body temperature. Otherwise, you would quickly become overheated and die. I sometimes think that homeostatic reflexes are at work in interpersonal relationships, too. When you change the dance, it's likely that your conflict partner will do everything possible to maintain the old beat, no matter how damaging the relationship has been for both of you. In fact, you may find her escalating her behavior in ways that make the conflict even worse. Don't let this surprise you.

Tim raced out of one of our workshops, bursting with motivation and determined to conquer his conflict on the very first try. A day later, we heard his deflated voice on the telephone. "She kept saying I wasn't a good listener, so I tried out my new listening skills and *IT DIDN'T WORK.* She looked right at me and said, 'What kind of garbage is that?'" Tim was all ready to fall right back into the old patterns that were making him so miserable. "Oh well, at least I tried," he sighed. "I guess she doesn't care about our relationship after all."

If you find yourself accused of weird behavior because you're attempting to change the dance, be honest about what's going on, and don't hide what you're trying to accomplish. Here are some possible responses:

- *This relationship is important to me. You've told me you don't think I'm a very good listener, so I'm trying to do better. If I seem phony to you, it's because this is new for me and I'm feeling very clumsy right now.*

- *I've just read a book on conflict management and have discovered, to my chagrin, that I may be a big part of the problem. I'm going to be trying out some new techniques and I'd appreciate your feedback on how I'm doing. Just don't laugh too hard, okay?*

- *You and I haven't gotten along very well in the past. It's been hard on me and I've been pretty upset by our arguments. I'm trying to behave in a different way, because I think it's important to the company for us to work better*

*together. If you don't understand what I'm doing, please
ask me. I'd like to talk to you about it.*

You'll never be recognized as a good listener if you only
listen once and then quit. Nor will all aspects of your conflict
be reconciled in one easy step. Moving from conflict to compatibility is not a one-shot deal. It's a long-term process that
can seem agonizingly slow in its execution, and you'll probably stumble along the way. It's also way too easy to become
self righteous, as Tim did, and blame your partner for not
responding exactly as you'd like. If you trust the process and
take it step by step, and if you're honest with your conflict
partner about your motives, you'll make haste slowly. But
your progress will always be in the right direction.

6

Step One: Analyze Your Conflict

The key to all good analysis is detachment—the ability to step back and view a situation or event with complete objectivity. Taped to my office telephone are these words: "Not only has one to do one's best, one must, while doing one's best, remain detached from whatever one is trying to achieve." This quotation has been stuck to my phone so long I've forgotten who said it and where I first heard it. Still, it remains a strong reminder to me that when I'm able to stay slightly detached from an issue, I'll do better than if I allow myself to get all tied up in knots.

To gain the insights that come from good analysis, you will be required to look at your conflict from the viewpoint of a disinterested bystander, almost as if you hired yourself as a consultant to come in and give you a fresh perspective. Eventually, you'll look hard at your own interests/needs, as well as those of your conflict partner. But for now I'll ask you to set them aside with the assurance that they won't be ignored forever.

The power of scripting

Is there a conflict from your past that still haunts you? Do you repeat its arguments over and over in your mind?

*And then he said, and then I said, and then he had the nerve to say, and then I **should** have said, and if I had said that, then he would have . . .* and the old tapes rewind themselves and play on and on into eternity. One way to rid your mind of those seemingly never ending battles is to write them down, turning your conflict event into a scene from a play. Once the words are on paper, their power to torment you will disappear, and the "shoulda-oughtas" floating around inside your head can be reserved until you're ready to strategize. Scripting your conflict is the first step to both detachment and successful analysis. It gives you something concrete with which to start.

Here are two examples of conflict scripts, both of which were submitted by workshop participants. As you write your script, you may find it much longer or much shorter than either of these examples. What's important in scripting isn't the length of the script but the accuracy of the wording, so be honest. Write down exactly what was said and done, with no editorializing to make yourself look better.

* Toby has been meaning to call Pam, but unexpectedly runs into her on the elevator.

    Toby: *Pam, can I come talk to you for a few minutes later this afternoon?*

    Pam: *About what?*

    Toby: *About the reimbursement problem.*

    Pam: *I don't know what's left to discuss. You aren't getting more than $10 for dinner and you know it.*

    Toby: *That part's not the problem. I just didn't like you using my name and implying that I'm behind all the fuss.*

    Pam: *You know the rules and you're getting time and a half, which is more than generous. I get so sick of people trying to take advantage. Everybody just thinks they can manipulate the system any way they want. Well, they can't do that to me.*

Toby: *Gee, Pam, I don't think it was a matter of manipulation. It was just a case of having to eat dinner. . .*

Pam: *But people just go out and order the most expensive things on the menu. That's just plain greedy.*

Toby: *Well, I'm not greedy. Considering that I worked until 4:00 in the morning, I don't think it was excessive. If the offer was made that I could eat anything on the menu, I don't see where I did anything wrong.*

Pam: *Well, you're part of that same group of people that's always trying to get something. A dinner break at time and a half is never enough, is it? You wouldn't eat that way at home.*

Toby: *I didn't charge for the time I went to dinner.*

Pam: *That doesn't matter; all this greediness has got to stop.*

Toby: (flustered) *This really isn't the place to discuss this.*

Pam: *Well,* **you're** *the one who wanted to talk. This isn't* **my** *fault.*

- Jill is at Mike's place, where they are preparing dinner.

Mike: *Hey, Jill, slice up my eggs, will ya?*

Jill: (setting the table) *Who was your servant last year? Can't you see I'm busy?*

Mike: *Well, you made the salad. Why in the heck didn't you just slice the eggs then? They go in the salad.*

Jill: *But I'm not making the salad now. I'm busy with something else.*

Mike: *Well, I'm sorry, but it didn't seem all that important.*

Jill: *You never think **anything** I do is important. I'll have you know that what I do is just as important as what you do. I'm not someone's serving girl.*

Mike: *I'm just as busy as you are. I've got the meat to finish. Besides, if you were my wife, you'd do it. Why do I always end up the bad guy?*

Jill: *I'm not your wife, I never **will** be your wife, and if you want eggs in your salad, you can just slice them yourself.*

Take your time preparing the script. Go back and relive the event, writing it down exactly as it occurred. If you begin to experience the anger and frustration of the original moment, try to distance yourself enough that your feelings don't block your play writing activities. When you're satisfied that your script is as accurate as you can make it, consider it as you answer these questions.

What is the substance of the conflict?

What was the argument actually about? When I asked Jill that question, she stated that the issue was that Mike kept ordering her around as if she were his slave or, worse yet, his mother. Mike insisted they were fighting about Jill's selfishness and the fact that she is "too independent for her own good." They were both wrong. For Mike and Jill, the substance issue is simply, *what's going to happen to the eggs?* For Pam and Toby, the situation is a bit murkier. Who gets charged what for dinner seems to be part of it, and there's a clear lack of up-front agreement on how Toby is expected to behave when he's out on a job at mealtime. But Toby merely wanted to consult Pam about the reimbursement problem. He wasn't expecting a confrontation, and her vehement response caught him by surprise.

What are the relationship issues?

The conflict between Mike and Jill is really about their

relationship. The eggs are incidental. In fact, Mike and Jill often play out the same conflict over other, diverse substance issues: the choice between a movie and a ball game, whose turn it is to pick up the cleaning, and whose family to visit over Thanksgiving. Some researchers believe that a conflict recurring three times without resolution has nothing much to do with content and everything to do with the relationship. Mike and Jill both drop verbal clues that tell us this is indeed the case.

> Jill: You never think *anything* I do is important. I'm not someone's serving girl.
>
> Mike: Why do I *always* end up the bad guy?

Pam and Toby aren't quite as tightly linked as the other couple. The relationship between Mike and Jill is a personal one, while Pam and Toby are business colleagues. Even though the substance issues appear to take precedence, Pam's emotional outburst indicates there's more going on here than just meal reimbursement, and the relationship between the two will need attention if they are to work together comfortably.

So Mike and Jill will need to think carefully about their relationship if they want to become more compatible, while Pam and Toby need to iron out their substance difficulties without damaging further a somewhat precarious, albeit more distant, relationship.

What sort of movie or TV show would your conflict be?

It's often helpful to visualize your conflict dramatized on the screen. Who plays you, and who plays your partner? What physical characteristics do they each have? What kind of voices? What is the atmosphere on the set—bright, lively, and energetic? Or dark and brooding? Jill imagined a situation comedy where both players engaged in constant one-upmanship, their bickering humorous to the audience but hurtful to the participants. The "happy" ending of each

episode left the audience engulfed in laughter, but the fade
out on the "Jill" character always showed her smiling
brightly to hide her tears.

Toby said he felt like the pink battery bunny—innocent
and without malice—marching along to the beat of his own
drum. "But," he said, "the hammer always misses the real
bunny, while I seem to get clobbered."

Another way to get a clearer understanding of your conflict is to describe it metaphorically. A metaphor is the defin-
ing of one thing by describing the qualities of another. I have
used a dance metaphor through this book to describe the
patterns of behavior that surround a conflict. One client
described her conflict as a coffee percolator. "We bubble
around until our tempers boil over, then we just sort of stop
and cool off. The quiet feels really good, but pretty soon
everything gets stale, and then one of us will start something
(brew another pot)."

What did you feel?

What were your feelings during the conflict?
Afterwards? List the negative emotions you felt: anger,
hatred, frustration, hurt, etc. Then create a sentence for each
emotion that begins: I felt (the emotion) because . . . . *I felt
left out because my work wasn't recognized in the staff meeting. I felt frustrated because I kept trying to make my point
and no one would listen. I felt embarrassed because I lost my
temper in front of the committee.* If you find that most of
your sentences begin, "I felt anger because . . . ," check yourself to see if you're feeling other, deeper emotions that mask
themselves as anger.

In the same way, analyze your conflict script to see if any
positive emotions happen to have been present. You may be
surprised to discover that you're perpetuating the conflict
because there's a psychological payoff for you. *I felt ener-
gized when I stood up to her. I felt superior because I was
able to show him I was right.* Conflicts get locked into pat-

terns because both parties gain something from the dance. There's something "in it" for each partner.

A friend of mine was addicted to high drama. He deluded himself by saying he wished he could resolve his conflict, but in reality he fed on the emotional meetings, the soul-searching letters, and the long lunches spent "getting everything worked out." The adrenaline rush that comes with emotional peaks and valleys can be habit forming, and for some people the high drama of conflict becomes a preferred way of life.

Where were you on the Balanced Communicator™ seesaw?

Were you to the left of the board, to the right, or balanced in the middle? Was your behavior appropriate to the situation? If you maintained an appropriate balance, you were able to take a good, hard look at the problem and yet pay attention to the needs of the relationship by remaining pleasant, open, and tactful during the altercation. But chances are that, because your conflict hasn't been resolved, you either tried to force your way through to a conclusion or you backed down and gave in to the demands of your partner. If your tendency is to reside more to the right of the *Balanced Communicator™* board without the equalizing of pressure on the other side, you can easily tilt far to the right and become rude, overpowering, and controlling—the seesaw crashing to the ground with the heavy weight of your behavior. If you favor the more accommodating left side of the bar, you could be playing the victim's role far more than you think.

Who has the power?

The struggle for power is a key component in all relationship conflicts. People often view power as finite; that is, there is only so much power to go around and if you have it, there won't be any left for me. In other words, one person's gain is the other's loss. A more constructive philosophy is that power resides within each one of us, and we lose it only when we give it up to someone else. Remember Brenda and Jane? Brenda relinquished her power when she avoided telling Jane she was busy with her own work. Even though she blamed Jane for being insensitive, the anger she felt afterwards actually stemmed from her own feeling of powerlessness.

Participants in VOICE-PRO workshops often report that they're in conflict with their bosses. As we get into conversations about their responsibility in the relationship and the actions they can take to manage the conflict, we hear a recurring theme: *But he (she) has all the power. I would never dare take that kind of initiative.* Their assumption is that they have no power or control over the situation. But there are no victims, remember? The positive role you play in any organization contributes directly to its success. No matter what its size, the organization wouldn't be the same without you, and because of your knowledge and expertise, you have within you a personal power that can and will impact your management of all your conflicts.

One way you can spot a power struggle is by noting whether one, or both, of you draws a third party into the fray. If you require allies to bolster your courage and support your position, you are trying to adjust what you perceive as an imbalance of power by acquiring more clout.

Was your conflict event a battle over power? Who grabbed it and who gave it away? Who controlled the conversation? Was there a shift in the power balance as the argument progressed? Are either of you gathering allies and, by doing so, creating opposing camps? Look carefully at your conflict and see if you can spot moments when the two of you were jockeying for power.

Is the fight about interests or needs?

Earlier we defined conflict as the struggle over opposing interests, wants, needs, or drives. It's important here to note the vast differences between needs/drives and interests/wants.

A need is something that's required for your well-being, something that you can't live without; it becomes a drive when there's an urgent or instinctual basis to the need. An interest (or want) is something that's desirable. I *need* a job; I *want* to be a manager. You *need* to provide for your family; your desire to provide them with a big house in the suburbs, designer clothes, and expensive vacations is a very big *want*. Self-esteem is a *need*; power over others is a *want*. To preserve the relationship, Jill needs to feel valued by Mike as a human being. Setting the table and slicing the eggs aren't needs; they're just tasks. Wanting something desperately doesn't automatically turn it into a need. Like a dictator's desire for power, an Olympic athlete's quest for the gold is still a *want*— even though the athlete may have turned it into an obsession.

Confusing your needs with your interests can become a huge disadvantage for you at negotiation time. In your analysis, distinguish carefully between what you'd like, what you want, and what you actually need.

Is this a single or a repetitive incident?

Is your scripted conflict an isolated incident or a scene in a longer play? Pam's outburst may be the result of a simple misunderstanding, or she may just be having a bad day. On the other hand, a dance may be going on here. Toby timidly asks a question . . . Pam jumps all over him. . . Toby half-heartedly defends himself . . . Pam persists . . .Toby retreats. Jill imagines her conflict as a situation comedy with ongoing installments that always play out the same way, which indicates that her conflict is clearly episodic. A large number of episodes will dictate a requirement for greater emphasis on relationship issues as your conflict management proceeds. If you determine your conflict scenario is a repetitive one, note whether the substance remains the same or is modified with each episode. Also, take a look at how your behavior continues to reinforce the pattern, no matter how the content changes.

Just how important is this conflict, anyway? You may decide to chalk an isolated incident up to misunderstanding and let it go at that. Be careful, however, that you don't let too many incidents go by unchallenged. If the results of your Proverbs test indicated that either denial or accommodation is your *style* rather than an occasional response, you'll want to examine the importance of the conflict to you more precisely. "Choosing your battles" and "not sweating the small stuff" may be good strategies, but they may just as easily be cop-outs.

Are there unwritten rules that perpetuate the conflict?

Written rules are easy. They have substance; you can discuss them, argue over them, even change them if you like. Unwritten rules are deadly shadows. Everyone knows they're there, but they're never, ever acknowledged:

- Daddy is drunk every night, but no one is to talk about it.
- The boss's 10-year-old daughter comes in every Saturday, uses Mary's desk to "play secretary," and never puts anything away, but Mary doesn't dare mention it.
- No one in the group can talk about George's poor performance, because to complain means you're not a team player.

If you try to bring an unwritten rule out into the open, you're likely to get blank stares and uncomfortable silences, because no one wants to own up to being influenced by something that isn't really there. Are there unwritten rules underlying your conflict? What are your perceptions of what's allowed and what isn't? Did any of this influence your behavior during the event? Your acknowledgment of the presence of unwritten rules is the first step in safely bringing them out into the open.

What is your conflict partner's viewpoint?

This is the hardest part of your analysis. Think about how your conflict partner would have written your script. I recently heard the description of a family conflict as told by four family members who were directly involved in the fight. The substance of the conflict was crystal clear to all of them, because almost word for word, I heard the same story from each participant. Their interpretations of the relationship issues, however, were quite different.

What would your conflict partner say about the substance of the conflict? How would she describe the relationship? Answer all the questions again, this time in your partner's words. Jill's reverse analysis might start out something like this: *Mike likes to coordinate his cooking so everything is done at the same time. He was finishing up the meat and got flustered because he realized the eggs weren't in the salad. He didn't stop to think about what I was doing. He was just thinking about the eggs.*

Jill will make a big mistake if she funnels Mike's viewpoint through her own eyes. *Mike never thinks about anyone but himself, so when he saw the eggs weren't sliced, he ordered me to stop what I was doing and serve him—the great chef of the world.* The objective is to gain insight into the conflict by putting yourself in the other person's shoes and thinking like he did. This doesn't mean you're obligated to agree with his viewpoint; it does mean you have to do your best to understand it.

Summary

When you analyze your conflict, you'll gain a dispassionate view of the event and the larger pattern of which it may be a part. The very process of scripting the event will help you let go of the replays that haunt you and will provide you with much-needed objectivity. Answer these questions from both your own point of view and that of your conflict partner:

1. What is the substance of the conflict?
2. What are the relationship issues?
3. What sort of movie or TV show would your conflict be?

4. What did you feel?
5. Where were you on the *Balanced Communicator*™ see-saw?
6. Who has the power?
7. Is the fight about interests and wants or needs and drives?
8. Is this a single or repetitive incident?
9. Are there unwritten rules that perpetuate the dance?
10. What is your conflict partner's viewpoint?

Carolyn, I don't have to write all of this down, do I?

Of course not. If it's helpful to write down your thoughts, by all means do so, but as long as you've scripted out your conflict scenario, you're okay. Take a long walk, go for a drive, or sit on a beach and think through your answers to the questions, some of which will be more relevant to you than others. Let your mind wander. The insights will come when you're ready for them. Then you can begin to set some goals.

7

Step Two: Determine Your Goals and Priorities

If you're trapped in the repetitive patterns of a conflict, it's all too easy to be oblivious to the opportunities for peace that are available to you. Clear goals are the drivers for change that will move you and your partner out of the state of conflict and into one of compatibility. You'll need to establish a clear picture of what your situation would be like if the conflict disappeared—a "wish list," if you will, for you and your partner. You'll then need to turn that picture into a series of goal statements that will redirect your efforts onto a new path and eventually into a new pattern. You'll need to establish short-term and long-term goals, which address both the substance and relationship issues of your conflict. In addition, because conflict often erupts suddenly and catches you by surprise, you'll many times be required to make quick decisions about your "in-the-moment" priorities.

The value of goals

Good goals will tell you where you want to go. They will help you focus on a workable solution to the problem and assure you a process for handling future conflict episodes. They will take your interests/needs into account and address those of your conflict partner. Good goals will help you avoid further damage to fragile relationships and create immensely satisfying, long-lasting partnerships.

I can't stress enough the importance of *Step Two* in your approach to managing conflict. Goal setting gives you foresight, so when the time comes, you know how to "fight the good fight." Without this step, you're apt to react mindlessly to provocation and do and say things for which you'll be very sorry.

Clear goals pave the way for the right action. Imagine that you're the parent of a 16-year-old son. (If you *are* the parent of a teenager, this will be easy.) The two of you have been at odds for some time, and the situation has deteriorated since he's reached driving age. For weeks he's been badgering you to give him the car on Saturday night, and after a long holdout, you have reluctantly given in—with the stipulation that he will be home by midnight. At 2:30 AM you're frantic. You're pacing the floor, visions of bloody collisions dancing in your head, when you hear the car drive in. Racing to the garage, you discover a sizable dent in the back fender; and when you confront your son, he flips you the keys and heads for the stairs.

Okay, what do you do now? Under these circumstances, your first impulse may be to blow up—raging about how you knew he would come to a bad end, accusing him of being the most untrustworthy kid on earth, and grounding him till he's twenty-one. Hold it—time out for goal setting. Your immediate priority is to cool off and not make the situation worse, so first of all, block your impulse to go into a tirade and instead declare a truce until tomorrow. This will give you time to figure out your short-term goal, which will probably be something like: *make sure this incident doesn't repeat itself and that when my son makes a promise, I know he will honor it.*

Giving in to your initial impulses will generate actions that lead you away from your desired result, not toward it.

Without taking a timeout for goal setting, you will further damage an already stormy relationship, and your energies will then be spent patching things up rather than embarking on your long-term goal: *to build a lasting relationship with your son based on mutual love, respect, and trust.*

Clear goals help you evaluate your progress. If you don't know what you want, you won't recognize it when you get it. People in the throes of conflict will often argue vehemently over an issue in which they are in total agreement. They don't recognize the fact that they're saying the same thing, only in different words. If your goals are clear, you'll recognize 1) when you're moving in the right direction, 2) when you're off the track, and 3) when you're simply spinning your wheels.

Clear goals will get you there. Clear goals are more achievable than vague ones. People work harder to achieve goals they can understand. Otherwise, without thorough comprehension of the desired result, they continue to muddle around. For instance:

- *I want to develop a schedule with Brenda, so I know when it's convenient for her to help me with my typing and when it's not.* . . . is more doable than . . . *I wish Brenda would stop getting mad at me when I ask her to do something.*
- *I want to clarify the reimbursement policy so my expense sheets will fit within the guidelines* . . . is more doable than . . . *I've got to be careful that I don't set Pam off every time I want information.*
- *I want to develop a professional life independent of my marriage* . . . is more doable than . . . *I want my spouse to respect me more.*

We've been talking throughout this chapter about immediate priorities and short-term and long-term goals. Let's look at each of these in more detail.

What is your priority?

In order to qualify for a highly specialized project, Claire, an architect, arranged a joint venture with Hank, a consultant who had expertise in the needed area. Together they worked out a strategy for landing the job—a strategy that included an on-site rehearsal of the presentation they would make to the client's board of directors. When rehearsal time came, not only did Hank arrive late, he came unprepared, thus wasting everyone's time and jeopardizing the project by botching a much-needed practice session. In addition, when Claire suggested a quick run through before the actual presentation, Hank begged off, pleading a former engagement. Claire and her partners were furious and in their anger let loose all sorts of "suggestions" for how to deal with Hank: *kick him off the project . . . call him at 2:00 AM to "see if he's practicing" . . . put up a billboard in the center of town that reads, "Hank lets people down" . . . snub him at the interview so he'll feel guilty . . . .*

Fortunately, a cooler head prevailed. Claire interrupted this diatribe with the words, "Hey, guys, let's remember that our priority is to get this job. We'll need to redesign the presentation so Hank's part is smaller. That way, he won't do us too much damage, but he'll still be a part of it. The client needs see us as a team, even if we don't feel that way right now. If we get the job, we'll deal with our relationship with Hank; if we don't get the job, we'll know not to partner with him again. But in the meantime, we've got work to do, so let's get going."

Conflict can strike when and where you least expect it. The problem with being blind-sided is that it tends to cloud your thinking so you get dragged down into the controversy, your energies drawn away from the real issue. Claire could easily have fed her frustration by grumbling her way through the presentation and letting the client see her anger at Hank. Indeed, until she intervened, her team preoccupied itself with thinking up spiteful acts of revenge against Hank. But by asking herself the question, "What is my priority?", she was able to put her resentment aside and concentrate on the team's immediate goals—giving a good presentation and impressing the client.

Let's look back at the Toby/Pam scenario in Chapter 6. When Toby met Pam in the elevator, his opening words to her were, "Pam, can I come talk to you for a few minutes later this afternoon?" He didn't expect Pam to get angry and was unprepared for her outburst, in large part because the elevator was the wrong venue for the discussion. Here's how the scene might have played if Toby had stopped and asked himself, "What is my priority?"

Toby: *Pam, can I come talk to you for a few minutes later this afternoon?*

Pam: *About what?*

Toby: *About the reimbursement problem.*

Pam: *I don't know what's left to discuss. You aren't getting more than $10 for dinner and you know it.*

Toby: (to himself, ". . . my priority? To set up a meeting") *Perhaps not, but I do have some concerns I'd like to clear up. If I stop up around 4:00, would that be all right?*

Toby can tell from Pam's words and her tone of voice that she's feeling testy, but he now has the time to set his own goals and plan a strategy that will lead to a far more productive meeting than their original confrontation in the elevator. In the heat of the moment, when tempers flare, *STOP!* Ask yourself, "What is my priority?" This technique will give you time to think and prevent you from doing or saying something you'll later wish you hadn't.

Short-term and long-term goals

Claire's immediate priority was to give a good team presentation, regardless of how well or poorly Hank played his part. Upon receiving a contract from the client, her short-term goal would become: *Clarify the roles and responsibilities of each team member, so an incident like this doesn't occur again.* (This is a content goal.) Her long-term goal would be to: *Build a mutually beneficial partnership with Hank, so we can continue to collaborate on special projects and together create a new market niche.* (This is obviously a relationship goal.) In the event the team *didn't* get the job, the short-term goal might change to: *Sever the relationship without acrimony;* and the long-term goal: *keep the door open for future possible alliances.*

Let's imagine that Pam delays Toby's request for a meeting until the end of the week. This gives Toby time to think about what he wants to accomplish when they get together. Here's a memo to Pam from Toby, laying out his agenda.

> *Pam—*
> *I'm looking forward to Friday's meeting. At that time, I hope we can clarify the dinner reimbursement policy so my expense sheets will be accurate when I submit them to you. I'd also like to make sure we're in agreement about how to communicate in the future, so this kind of misunderstanding doesn't happen between us again. I enjoy working with you and would like to make these situations easier on both of us. See you Friday.*
> *—Toby*

In this memo, Toby clearly states his short-term objective, which is to clarify the reimbursement policy. He then looks for ways to improve his and Pam's long-term relationship by working out a dispute resolution process for the future. He deals with the content as well as the relationship aspects of the conflict, and he even suggests that a simple misunderstanding was the cause of the original argument.

Toby has openly articulated his interests/needs and at the same time has avoided even the hint of suspicion, exasperation, or blame against Pam.

Goals can change

Since flexibility is a key component of our *Balanced Communicator*™ seesaw, keep in mind that, as your management of the conflict progresses, your goals could change. Your preliminary goal setting will only take you so far. You'll be acquiring new or additional information and will need to weigh that new information against your original goals, adapting them as you go along.

What if, upon storming into the garage to confront your "irresponsible" son, you discover him sitting, exhausted and distraught, in the driver's seat. He tells you that, on his way home at 11:30, he witnessed that bloody collision you had been angrily envisioning. He then spent the next few hours finding help, holding a frightened toddler in his lap while waiting for the emergency crew, and giving his statement to the police. By the time he was allowed to leave the scene, he was so tired that he inadvertently backed into a light pole and dented the fender.

Your son's explanation of his whereabouts between midnight and 2:30 AM changes your outlook by giving you information you didn't have before. The lateness of the hour isn't an issue any longer, and he has proved his trustworthiness and sense of responsibility. Instead of buying time for a cooling off period, your immediate priority in this scenario changes to: *provide comfort and protect the relationship.* So you listen to your son's story, tell him you're proud of him, and send him off to bed. Your actions change because your immediate priority has changed. Tomorrow you address your short-term goals: dealing with the dented fender and working out a plan whereby he lets you know if an emergency has delayed him.

In less dramatic fashion, let's say I want a raise, and since employers never seem to want to give raises, I'm arming myself for battle. My goals for the meeting are to get the raise and to prove to him how valuable I am and how much the company would suffer if it were to lose me. Data in hand, I march into his office, but before I even open my mouth, he says, "Carolyn, I know you want to talk to me about a raise. I want to tell you that you certainly deserve one. Your work has significantly improved the company's bottom line, everyone around here likes you, and I consider you one of our best people. Unfortunately, building that new plant has strapped us for cash, and there will be no raises this year . . . for anyone."

Oops, time to change goals. My employer has preempted me with his validation of my worth to the company; there's no argument there. He flat-out said no raises and he always means what he says, so I guess I'd better save my debate for another time. The new goals? Explore the possibilities of alternate forms of compensation and keep the door open for further discussions about the raise as cash flow improves.

Next steps

So, *Step Two* for the management of your conflict is to determine your goals and priorities. To do this, picture in your mind what it would be like to have your conflict resolved once and for all. Now, using the chart on the following page, turn your picture into a series of goal statements. Do you have immediate priorities that must be addressed right now? If so, list them. Make sure you give equal consideration to both the substance (content) and relationship aspects of your situation. Then think about the results you'd like in the very near future and those that will take time to accomplish. Write them down. Remember, to be effective, your goals must help you to:

- achieve a workable solution to the problem
- meet your own interests/needs
- address the interests/needs of your conflict partner
- develop a process for handling future conflict episodes

Substance (Content) Goals	Relationship Goals
Immediate priority:	Immediate priority:
Short-term:	Short-term:
Long-term:	Long-term:

Carolyn, do I have to fill in each block?

No, individual conflicts are unique, so no hard and fast rules pertain to how you set your own goals. Just give careful thought to each category. That way you won't miss anything that could influence your actions later on.

8

Step Three: Keep Your Cool, Keep Your Power

Up to this point, you've done a lot of thinking about conflict. You've looked at the nature of conflict, and I hope by this time you've come to the conclusion that it can be a constructive influence in your life. You've seen that you can ignore neither the substance nor the relationship elements of your conflict. You've looked carefully into your own "knee-jerk" responses to conflict to determine if you have a single conflict style that's always operative or if you're more versatile and respond according to each given situation. You've also worked through *Step One* and *Step Two* of our process and have analyzed your scripted conflict, set your goals, and determined your priorities. Your logical, analytical mind has been at work; you've gained awareness and insight, and you're well on your way to already managing your conflict better than you've ever done before.

Also, up to this point, you've been able to work on your own, disengaged from the conflict itself and without the need to interact with other people. This is about to change. While this detachment has given you time for reflection and planning, the time is coming for you to address your concerns to your conflict partner. So ready or not, you're about to find yourself in a . . . **CONFRONTATION**.

Confrontation is scary

When I coach clients on how to deal with conflict and their moment of confrontation approaches, I invariably hear the words, "I *hate* this." These words are accompanied by sighs, shudders, grimaces, and other nonverbal signals of resignation and dread. Even the word *confrontation* conjures up images of hostility—the violent clashing of forces and ideas that sets the adrenaline pumping and floods the body with dreadful, out-of-control feelings.

Rational thought and emotional thought occur in two different places in the brain. It's all one brain, but it can be helpful for our purposes to suspend reason and to imagine that you actually have two brains: the logical brain that thinks—providing you with the ability to mull things over, ponder, muse, reflect, consider, contemplate, decide, and interpret—and the emotional brain that feels—telling you what you like and don't like, what pleases you, what thrills you, what causes you anguish, and what you fear. Feelings that were generated by past events in your life live on in the depths of your emotional brain, although the events themselves may be long forgotten. The stronger, more emotionally charged the original event, the more indelible the latent feelings. These feelings can surface in response to a current event, such as your present conflict, and can influence your behavior without you even knowing why.

For example, I get mad when I hurt myself; a stubbed toe or pinched finger fills me with rage, which is a totally inappropriate response to accidental pain. Backaches and headaches don't upset me, but if you inadvertently whack me with a tennis ball, I'll be furious. When my mother once tried to comfort me after I chewed up my finger in the ice crusher, I lashed out at her. This hurt her feelings; she accused me of being insensitive, and we ended up in a big fight, while I bled all over the kitchen floor. (Not the best way to foster a close relationship.) This irrational anger comes from somewhere deep down inside me. Why? I haven't a clue. It's just there, popping up at the worst possible moments. When people push your "hot buttons," they're touching those emotional private places where your old hurts and fears reside.

Your emotional brain is what triggers the famous "flight or fight" response, where the onslaught of adrenaline and other hormones brings about complex and powerful changes in your body. In "flight or fight" mode, your heart rate increases, sometimes as much as thirty beats per minute. As your blood pumps faster, your blood vessels constrict, trying to compensate in order to maintain their efficiency. This constriction shuts down organs not necessary for doing battle, which explains why your stomach may feel queasy as blood is redirected from the gastrointestinal tract to your heart and skeletal muscles in preparation for quick action. In your lungs, the bronchial tubes expand and you breathe faster. You may even feel out of breath as your body strives to take in more air. Salivary secretion declines, often resulting in a dry mouth, but the moisture has to go somewhere, so you break out in a sweat. All over your body, your muscles tighten. In earlier times, extreme muscle tension made it more difficult for the spears of rival tribesmen to penetrate the skin and cause serious injury. Today, although your business colleagues aren't going to throw real spears, just the anticipation of their verbal attacks can cause the same primitive reactions.

Whether the confrontation is happening "in the moment" or is an anticipated event, it unleashes within us emotional and physiological responses that can be overwhelming, no matter how calm and logical we try to be. With this to look forward to, it's no wonder people find confrontation scary. Yet, face-to-face conversation is a necessary component of all conflict management, and you will either initiate the encounter yourself or it will be thrust upon you by circumstance. You will be at a decided advantage if your emotion-management skills keep your deepest feelings and your flight-or-fight instincts at bay.

Poise under pressure

Whether you're an athlete, a speaker, or a participant in a conflict scenario, you must be able to relax under pressure. If you get uptight just thinking about having an encounter with your conflict partner, you're not alone. The fear of losing your cool is a real one; blowing up, freezing into rigidity, or, worse yet, bursting into tears are all possibilities that will hurt your cause. Win or lose, your ability to stay calm is what allows you to think on your feet and make wise, in-the-moment decisions. You can improve your chances for a relaxed, easier encounter in four ways: be ready, loosen your muscles, breathe deeply, and maintain your focus.

Be ready. You've been preparing yourself for the encounter throughout this book as you've learned more about conflict and your responses to it. In addition, you must do your homework about the substance (content) of the conflict. If you want your marketing plan to be accepted and supported by your conflict partner, you'd better have costs and revenue projections at your fingertips. Build your case, anticipate questions that are likely to be thrown at you, and prepare the answers.

Be specific. If Brenda wants to build a better working relationship with Jane, she can't plop herself down in Jane's office and complain, "You always throw things at me to do at the last minute." She needs to fill in the details, even if she must delay the encounter until she has more precise information. "Seven times over the last month, you've asked me to help you with a project. Five of those were last-minute jobs and I've had to put aside my own work to help you out." Back up your arguments with supporting data. Generalizations like, "You don't respect me," and "You never listen," are unsupportable assumptions about another's motivations or feelings and will only make you look unprepared.

Loosen your muscles. As I write this, I'm watching Olympic swimmers loosen up before the 800-meter relay. Athletes know that when their bodies are relaxed, they'll perform better. You may not be involved in Olympic competition, but if you're able to bring your conflict to a successful conclusion, you'll feel like you've won a gold medal. To do this, you'll need command over your muscles, which in turn will give you greater presence of mind and emotion. Physical tension is blocked energy—energy that *must* be released. The tightness and shakiness that you experience during confrontation will get worse if you try to control it by holding it in. Olympic swimmers know the importance of releasing this kind of tension before an event. How do they do it? They shake loose. To the same end, we teach this simple relaxation exercise at the start of all our workshops, no matter what subject we're teaching.

> Stand with your feet shoulder-width apart. Begin by wiggling your fingers—just your fingers. Now add your hands and shake them, too. Add, one by one, your elbows, shoulders, chest, waist, hips, knees, and feet, until you're shaking all over. Let your head move with your body and add your voice to the action, shaking all the way down to your toes. Come slowly to a stop and let yourself settle. Check your shoulders to make sure they're still loose. Then breathe easily and deeply, down into your body.

Scanning is another technique that will help. When you understand your body's signals and know how to handle them, you'll be able to relax at will, loosening tense muscles and using the released energy for clear thinking and decision making. To do this, you need to recognize your "trouble

spots," those personal hiding places where you store excess
tension. Common trouble spots are the jaw, the back of the
neck, the shoulders, and the knees. Practice doing quick body
scans, using your inner awareness to pinpoint areas of tension, then have a silent conversation with the offending muscle, instructing it to "let go." This practice will require some
time and effort at first, but over time it will become quick
and automatic. When it does, you'll be able, in the midst of
your encounter, to recognize tight shoulders or a clenched
jaw and relax them at will. You'll have adjusted your body
for your own comfort, and no one will be the wiser.

   Breathe deeply. The best way of all to relax your body
and focus your mind is simply to breathe. Diaphragmatic, or
deep breathing is the oldest and still the most effective
stress-reducing technique known. It's been used for thousands of years to quell anxiety and promote a general state
of well-being. Many people think that deep breathing means
taking great big gulps of air, but the word "deep" actually
refers to positioning in the body. Here is another simple exercise. (You'll need an assistant the first couple of times you try
this. Then you'll be able to do it by yourself.)

> Sit upright in a straight chair. Ask your assis-
> tant to stand behind you and lean his forearms
> on your shoulders—lightly, so you feel the
> pressure but it's not painful. Take a big
> breath. If you feel an increased pressure of his
> arms on your shoulders, your breath is coming
> in too high. Take another breath, this time
> sending it deeper into your body, so the pres-
> sure on your shoulders is reduced and you feel
> the expansion in the area around and just
> above your waist.

   Repeat this exercise several times a day, increasing the
amount of air you take in with each breath, always monitor-
ing your shoulders to keep them down and relaxed.

Remember, a deep breath is one that is placed deep in your body; it's not a huge gasp that fills your upper chest.

Maintain your focus. Stay focused on the goals you've set for yourself. Studies have shown that, in ordinary, garden-variety business meetings, the topic of conversation changes about every ninety seconds. This shows how easy it is to get side-tracked, even when emotions aren't running high. In a conflict scenario where issues *are* emotional, your conflict partner, feeling threatened, may counter with a deliberate change of subject.

> You: *Mary, your last project was completed two months late and ran 15 percent over budget. This new project of yours will need to be tightened up.*
>
> Mary: *Well, I had a lot of other work to do, and I did the best I could. Besides, Tom's project was even later than mine, and you didn't say anything to him.*
>
> You: *Mary, I try to be fair. I talked to Tom about that, but there were some extenuating circumstances that made it impossible for him to stay on schedule.*
>
> Mary: *That's not fair. I deserve the same consideration Tom gets. Why, he even . . . .*

. . . and now you're in the muck. The issue is no longer Mary's project; it's been successfully switched, by Mary, to general issues of fairness and—even more off point—your relationship with Tom. Let's rewrite this script so your focus remains squarely on your goals.

> You: *Mary, your last project was completed two months late and ran 15 percent over budget. This new project of yours will need to be tightened up.*
>
> Mary: *Well, I had a lot of other work to do, and I did the best I could. Besides, Tom's project was*

> *even later than mine, and you didn't say any-thing to him.*

You: *This has nothing to do with Tom. Right now, I'm interested in finding out how you plan to finish the new project on time and keep it on budget.*

Mary: *That's not fair. Tom . . .*

You: *Mary, if there are legitimate reasons why you got behind on the last project, I want to hear them. Otherwise, let's look ahead and see how you can tighten up your schedule.*

Action! Then what?

Very often, your emotional brain engages first, with your thoughts following in a more methodical, and probably more accurate, way. Under stress, we tend to bypass rational thinking and react instinctively, without giving ourselves time to figure out what's really going on. *Action/reaction* occurs almost instantaneously. When I speak to groups of people about conflict, I often ask someone to hold her hand up, palm facing out. I put my palm against hers and push. Without thinking, my opponent almost always pushes back. In an emergency, when there's not time to think things through, this instinctive, "push back" response to a stimulus is great, because the adrenaline rush gives us courage, stamina, and a heightened awareness of what needs to be done. However, in normal, everyday interactions with people at work and at home, and especially in conflict situations, *action/reaction* equals trouble.

Let's add a couple of arrows and another word to our equation:

$$\text{action} \rightarrow \text{thought} \rightarrow \text{reaction}$$

Now, your conflict partner's action leads to your thought, which leads to your reaction. The "thought" step creates a buffer that will keep you from over-reacting, or reacting too fast. It momentarily disengages your emotional brain and allows your thinking brain to take over. One possible buffering "thought" is your question from the last chapter, "What is my priority?" Here are some other possibilities:

- Is this the appropriate time and place for us to discuss this?
- Count to 10.
- Is there anything I need to know before I respond?
- Take a deep breath.
- Relax those muscles.
- At this moment, am I thinking logically or acting emotionally?
- Is my conflict partner thinking logically or acting emotionally?

We'll talk more about the differentiation between logic and emotion in the next chapters. In the meantime, thinking before you react will give you greater control over your emotional life. Memorize this *action → thought → reaction* diagram. Write it down. Carry it alongside your card containing the statement, "I am responsible for the success of each and every one of my relationships." When you are pushed, don't push back . . . yet. Instead, take a moment to consider something . . . anything.

Stay open

If you keep your cool, you will keep your power. During your encounter, your conflict partner can't see what's going on inside your head, so you must convey your messages not only through words, but also through posture and body language. While I don't believe that a given physical gesture can or will telegraph a single, specific meaning, I *am* a proponent of the idea that posture and body language send strong messages about personal power that cannot be ignored.

Structure your posture and body language to take advantage of your positive personal characteristics and minimize your weaker ones, as they're described on the

Balanced Communicator™ seesaw. For instance, my energy, spirit, and enthusiasm usually come through loud and clear; I don't have to do anything extra to get those qualities across. To keep a good balance, however, I need to convey "cool." So I always sit back in my chair with an open posture, my arms resting lightly on the arms of the chair. I lean slightly to one side, since asymmetrical posture comes across as more casual than a squared-off position, and cross one leg over the other. Easy, comfortable, and . . . cool. In moments of stress when I feel myself wanting to surge forward into the other person's space, I tell myself, "Relax your shoulders, Carolyn, sit back in your chair, and stay open."

On the other hand, if your tendencies are more on the left side of the *Balanced Communicator*™ board, you may inadvertently send signals that say: *I don't want to be here.* Rounding your shoulders, scrunching down in your chair, crossing your arms tightly over your chest, and avoiding eye contact—all these broadcast your hope that, if you make yourself small enough, no one will see you. In this case, my advice is to sit up, look directly at your conflict partner, use strong gestures, speak with a firm voice, and stay open.

The key to strong body language is to stay open. If you're sitting or standing in an open position, you're signaling strength. It's as if you were proclaiming, "Go ahead and shoot your arrows. They can't hurt me. But if they do, I'm strong enough to take it." Incidentally, there's something magical about open posture, for when you look strong, you feel strong. And pretty soon that strength will become real.

It's okay to get mad

We've talked a lot about the damage out-of-control emotions can cause and how giving yourself time to think can help you keep your cool. Please don't get the idea that it's wrong to feel the anger, hurt, and frustration that have been evoked by your conflict situation, or that even if you are experiencing strong emotions, it's a mistake to let them show. Actually, the opposite is true. Research into the workings of the logical and emotional parts of the brain indicate that both are critical for good decision making and clear thinking. Besides, while the substance issues of your conflict will require precision of thought, when you attempt to clear up the relationship issues, you'll find you're dealing almost totally with emotions—yours and those of your conflict partner. If you can't acknowledge and validate what each of you is feeling, the relationship will suffer additional blows.

The key to keeping your cool is to *manage* your feelings so they become the guiding spirit that leads you into the state of compatibility that is your goal. If you deny your emotions or try to hold them in for too long, they could erupt at inopportune times, either substantially weakening your position or destroying all possibilities for a successful resolution. Your emotions are legitimate; they make you who you are, and they need to be expressed.

Summary

Sooner or later, you must engage your partner in a discussion of the conflict. This confrontation is frightening to many people because it generates not only strong emotions about the current situation but also dredges up deeply buried hurts and fears from the past. Your logical brain and your emotional brain work in concert to help you through the conflict resolution process—your logical brain supplying the analytical powers necessary for problem solving and your emotional brain giving you energy, spirit, caring, and judgement.

The skill of relaxing under pressure includes: doing your homework so you're ready for the encounter, keeping your muscles loose and ready for action, breathing deeply at all times, and maintaining a clear focus on your goals. In addition, you need to place a buffering thought between the stimulus of an attacking action and your response to it. By adding a strong, open posture and body language that addresses both sides of the *Balanced Communicator*™ see-saw, you'll make sure your nonverbal signals reinforce the meaning behind your words.

And finally, your emotions are as much a part of you and the way you communicate as your logical thought processes. Feelings play a legitimate role in the conflict management process and should never be denied.

9

Time Out!

Let's take a brief time out and give some thought to the location of your encounter. Ken Burns, the celebrated producer of the PBS documentary, *The Civil War*, said once in a speech, "Communication can only take place between equals." His point is worthy of consideration, because it illustrates the difficulty many people experience when they try to communicate across the hierarchal lines of an organization. For example, in order to please, a person will tend to say what he thinks his superior wants to hear. Normally, this is not conscious subterfuge, but a well-intentioned attempt to be upbeat and positive—a team player. So, in evaluating information, a prudent manager understands that good news is never as good as it appears and bad news is generally worse. Because of this, you can count on misunderstandings and misinterpretations in any conversation where concerns about rank or position exist.

Whatever the rank of your conflict partner—boss, peer, employee, parent, child, spouse, "significant other," you'll want to create an environment for your encounter that's conducive to open, honest discussion without fear. This means choosing a neutral site, one that generates a sense of equality rather than hierarchy. At work, choose a conference room or quiet lounge over either your conflict partner's office or your own.

You:	*There have been times recently when you and I seem to have been at odds, and I'd like to see if we can clear things up. Are you free to meet with me one day next week? I'll reserve the conference room so we won't be disturbed.*
Boss:	*What's the matter with right now? Sit down and we'll talk.*
You:	*I'd like to get my thoughts in order first, so I don't waste your time. And when we do meet, it's important for me to have your undivided attention. So if it's all right with you, I'll reserve the conference room.*

If you must meet in your office, a couch or chairs situated around a low coffee table is much more conducive to honest talk than a desk or table of regulation height. People are generally more comfortable conversing when they're sitting at approximate right angles to each other, so arrange your room accordingly. Don't barricade yourself behind your desk, especially if you happen to be the higher-ranking person. Remember, the objective is to create an "equality" environment so neither of you start off feeling like the underdog.

If your conflict centers more around the relationship than the content, take yourselves off site whenever possible. Since offering food is part of the human ritual of hospitality, you can level the psychological playing field by taking your conflict partner out to eat. If you are peers, going out for a beer at the corner tavern can work, as long as the spot you choose is quiet enough to talk. Eating and drinking together will relax you both and help break down the barriers that separate you, which is the main reason why off-site retreats are so valuable for work teams; people are able to drop their pretenses and let their real selves show. If you're in a restaurant, choose a table for four, even though there are only two of you. That way you can sit at right angles and avoid the competitive feelings that could arise if you're facing off at each other across the table.

Give yourself time. If either of you feel rushed, you're less likely to accomplish what you set out to do. Be firm about your needs, but stay pleasant and willing to accommodate.

> You: *I'll reserve the conference room for an hour and a half on Tuesday. We may not need that long, but at least we won't be rushed.*
>
> Boss: *We'll have to make it quick. I don't have a lot of time.*
>
> You: *I'd like to meet when you're not in such a hurry. I know you're busy, but if you can allow an hour and a half now, it should save time in the long run. Shall we stay with Tuesday, or would another day be better?*

In this way, you're letting your conflict partner know that you're 1) sincere in your desire to resolve the differences between you; 2) determined to manage the encounter so something real is accomplished; 3) not willing to be stonewalled; and 4) approaching the situation in a spirit of cooperation and concern. In effect, when you take the initiative to orchestrate the encounter in this way, you're taking responsibility for the success of the relationship.

10

Step Four: Listen Until You Understand

Although listening may be the simplest of the communication skills to understand intellectually, it is without a doubt the most difficult to master, and no one is quite sure why. Perhaps it's because traditional schools teach reading, writing, and speaking as stand-alone subjects. If somewhere a college or university is offering Listening 101, I haven't heard of it. In addition, listening appears to be a passive process, because the effort it requires is mostly mental. Listening *looks* easy. It demands, however, an incredible amount of concentration and self discipline.

Listening is the act of receiving and interpreting spoken messages, and if that were all, then it *would* be easy. But there's a lot more to it than that. To listen well means that you fully understand the message from the *speaker's* point of view and you accept the fact that, to the speaker, that point of view is valid. You will not be able to change the patterns that have joined you in conflict unless you understand what is in the heart and mind of your conflict partner. This isn't something you can guess, or assume, or jump to conclusions about. You can only find answers by listening to what your partner tells you, in both spoken and unspoken messages.

I say, "Let's not go to the game because it's going to rain."
You look out the window at a clear, cloudless, sunny day. If
you're like most people, you reply, "Whatsa matter, you
crazy? There's not a cloud in the sky. Come on, let's go to the
game." But if you're a good listener, you won't say anything
until you've considered: *Hmm, for some reason Carolyn is
convinced it's going to rain. It doesn't make sense to me, but
she must have a reason for her opinion. I'd better find out
why.* Listening is the procedure you will use to find out why
your conflict partner thinks and feels the way she does.

Before we go on, let's get one thing straight. Being a
good listener does *not* mean you are obligated to agree with
what you hear. Understanding your partner's position won't
weaken your own. Nor will it make you look like a wimp in
the eyes of all your friends. Maybe, in the process, new information will give you insights you didn't have before, and
you may come to think in new ways. But this won't happen
because you're weak; it will happen because the new information has made you smarter.

Facts or emotions?

A valuable first listening technique is that of determining
whether the words and actions of your partner are a result of
thinking or feeling. At times, people express themselves in
ways that sound perfectly logical but really derive directly
from their emotions. They pretend to say what they *think*,
but in reality they're hiding what they *want* to believe
behind the facade of logical argument.

- *This is a bad decision. If we go ahead with it, we'll have
  a disaster on our hands* . . . could really mean . . . *I'm mad
  because you didn't take my advice, and I hope you fall
  flat on your face.*
- *I'll do the Miami job. It requires a senior person and I
  know more about the client than anyone else* . . . could
  really mean . . . *If it's Florida in the wintertime, it's mine,
  no matter who the client is.*

- *He's a mean, ungrateful kid, and I'm not going to take it anymore...* could really mean ... *I'm terribly hurt by his attitude, so to protect myself, I'll punish him.*

A good listener tries to figure out whether the facts speak for themselves or if there are hidden emotional undertones. In essence, you have to learn to read between the lines of your conflict partner's argument. Here are some clues to look for:

The words are overstated. Overblown language is a sign of the emotions at work. Words like *always, never, best,* and *worst* need to be taken with a grain of salt. "Obviously, this will never work," she says. Obvious to her, maybe, but not necessarily to other people. It's quite possible the facts of the matter are being over-ridden by her feelings.

The actions are out of character. If, under normal circumstances, he's a laid-back kind of guy and suddenly he stiffens up and speaks through clenched teeth, you can be pretty certain that he's no longer his normal self, that something has happened to make him angry. His emotions are ruling his behavior, regardless of what he's saying.

The words say one thing, the behavior says something else. "It's all right," she says in her martyr's voice, dejected and forlorn. "I don't mind. It's no big deal." And as she flounces out of the room, her dramatic sigh of resignation says that, to her, it's a very big deal indeed. (And if you take her at her word and treat the issue as no big deal, you'll escalate the conflict—big time.)

These examples show how easily emotions can be camouflaged by the appearance of logical thought. To be a good listener, you need to become sensitive to these inconsistencies and change your listening tactics accordingly.

The tactics of listening

Good listening requires becoming completely involved—mentally, emotionally, and physically—in the listening process. By responding verbally *and* nonverbally to both the spoken and unspoken messages of your conflict partner, you'll provide vital feedback that lets him feel heard and understood. The tactics of listening can be used independently or combined for maximum effectiveness. The tactics include:

- Paraphrasing the content
- Reflecting your partner's emotions
- Reflecting your partner's nonverbal signals
- Asking questions and using "tell me more" statements
- Giving undivided attention.

Let's consider each one separately, and then we'll see how they all fit together in a complete listening package.

Paraphrasing the content

Paraphrasing is a good way to verify the content of the message. When you paraphrase, you're making sure the pictures match and that you and your conflict partner are talking the same language. If you remember, in Chapter 3 we listed unclear roles and responsibilities, differing expectations, and misunderstandings as major causes of conflict. These content-related causes can all be mitigated through the use of the paraphrasing technique—restating what you hear, or *think* you hear, in your own words.

Claire, the architect, telephones her client, G-Corp, to inquire about late payments. G-Corp is six months behind in payment of $19,000 on projects that Claire believes to have been satisfactorily completed. In a heated phone discussion, G-Corp says they do have problems with the completed work and aren't going to pay up. Claire asks for a meeting, so they can resolve their differences in person. Five people are present at the meeting (collectively referred to here as G-Corp).

Claire: *The reason we're all here today is to discuss why we haven't been paid since June.*

G-Corp:	(throwing down a sheet of paper with five items on it) *This is why.*
Claire;	*Let me make sure I understand you. The items on this list you just passed out to us are the reasons you haven't paid us since June?*
G-Corp:	*Actually . . . no . . . not all of these items are a problem. Some are more current, but I guess it's just 4 and 5.*
Claire:	*So . . . we can eliminate the first three items from your list of reasons why we haven't been paid. Correct?*
G-Corp:	*Well, yes . . . but there are still other items on this list.*
Claire:	*Okay, why don't we talk about the remaining two items, issue by issue.*
G-Corp:	*Item #4 deals with the duplication of charges as they are represented in your invoices to us. By our calculations we don't owe you this much.*
Claire:	*(without defensiveness) You think we have duplicated our charges?* They nod. *Show me what you're referring to as duplications.*

(After going through the invoices one by one, it's clear the G-Corp has misread them. The invoices accurately represent work completed and no duplications exist.)

Claire:	*So, referring back to your list, it appears there is only one item now in question. Am I correct in assuming that there are no other issues in question besides this one remaining on the list?*
G-Corp:	*Yeah . . . well . . . we had questions about whether this part of the project should even have been undertaken. We let you go ahead, but it really wasn't necessary.*
Claire:	*So, the only reason we haven't been paid since*

> *June is because you have reservations about*
> *the appropriateness of this activity described*
> *here in Item #5.*

G-Corp: *Yes.*

Claire: *As I look at the invoices, I see that Item #5*
amounts to $7,500. Does it look that way to
you?

G-Corp: *Yes.*

Claire: *Then, if $7,500 is the amount of money you're*
contesting, it looks like you would have no
problem with paying us the remaining
$11,500.

G-Corp: *(silence . . . then. . .) Well, we will agree to pay*
the $11,500. But this last item is important.

Claire: *It's important to both of us to clarify this item,*
just as we've done with the others. But I don't
have our notes on this particular item here
today. Let me go back and review them; then
we'll meet again and see what we can do to
resolve this last issue. In the meantime, if
you'll cut us a check for $11,500, I'll stop by
and pick it up on Friday. Agreed?

G-Corp: *Agreed.*

In this scenario, Claire accomplished a number of things. First of all, she didn't lose her cool. Remaining calm and composed, she treated the situation as a misunderstanding to be cleared up and not an attack on her integrity (which was how she actually felt). She didn't blame G-Corp or try to convince them they were wrong. She was in the driver's seat, leading them through the items, paraphrasing their comments, checking the accuracy of her assumptions, and giving them the opportunity to correct either her interpretation or their original statements, as it became necessary. She got her $11,500 and set the stage for resolving the issue of the other $7,500. And she did it all without succumbing to

G-Corp's angry attack—without pushing back when she was pushed.

When paraphrasing, don't exaggerate or understate what you hear; restate it as accurately as you can. Don't add information or leave anything out. Don't editorialize; you're not trying to be persuasive; you're just clarifying. And whatever you do, don't parrot. Claire would have given up her leadership role in the meeting had she merely echoed G-Corp's words:

> G-Corp: *Item #4 deals with the duplication of charges as they are represented in your invoices to us. By our calculations we don't owe you this much.*
>
> Claire: *So, item #4 deals with the duplication of charges in our invoices to you. By your calculations, you don't owe us that much, right?*

The parroting of entire phrases or sentences is terrible communication. It's a trick some people use to pretend they're listening. It's manipulative, it's phony, and it makes people mad. So don't do it. You can, however, reuse a word or two of your partner's original statement:

- "What's your best guess?"
  "My *best guess* is that we'll . . ."
- "You make me so mad."
  "What is it that I'm doing that *makes you so mad?*"
- "I really want that house, but we can't afford it."
  "It's hard when you *really want* something and financially it's out of reach."

This is not parroting; it's a way of using your partner's own words in your paraphrase so there's a sense of connectedness between the two of you.

Use phrases like: *If I'm hearing you correctly . . .; Let me make sure I understand. You're saying . . .; So, you think (or feel) . . ., is that right?* Listen to the content of what's being said, restate what you hear in your own words, and check with your conflict partner to make sure your interpretation is correct. Continue to clarify until you've got it right and your partner lets you know you've got it right.

Paraphrasing *before* the fact

One way to avoid a potential conflict caused by unclear expectations is to anticipate what your partner *might* say and paraphrase before the words are even spoken. A friend of mine did just that when he took a new position that necessitated his working directly under the CEO. This CEO was a dynamic, energetic go-getter, whom everyone admired for his ability to get things done. He had, however, one big fault; he chewed out his subordinates in public, thus gaining himself the reputation of "The Great Humiliator."

On the first day of his new job, my friend reported to the CEO's office, where he spoke assertively: "Brad, I've been thinking about what you might want from me as one of your staff, and this is what I think. One, you want my total loyalty to the company, knowing I will put its success and well-being ahead of my personal goals. Two, you want 150 percent of my effort, day in and day out. And three, you want honesty and integrity from me, so you can trust me to keep your confidences and tell you the truth as I see it. I pledge all of this to you; you can count on it. In return, I'm asking you to promise me that if you and I have a problem, you will take it up with me privately and not treat me to a public chastisement. Are we agreed?"

The CEO thought a moment, then held out his hand and said, "Agreed." Fifteen years later, my friend reported that not an angry word had ever been spoken between the two men and that their working relationship remained a harmonious one. By paraphrasing in this way *before* an unpleasant incident took place, my friend took a big risk, but it was one that paid huge dividends throughout his career with the company.

Reflecting your partner's emotions

We all want to be heard. Your conflict partner is no different. "I want you to recognize me as a valuable human being, understand my problems, and help me with what I'm trying to accomplish. I want you to accept me and not stand in judgment of who I am. And I want you to do all this without my having to work so hard to get it across to you."

It's not enough to recognize that your conflict partner feels differently about issues than you do. As Roger Fisher and William Ury so eloquently write in their extraordinary book on negotiation, *Getting to Yes* (Penguin Books, New York):

> ". . . you need to understand empathetically the power of their point of view and to feel the emotional force with which they believe in it. It is not enough to study them like beetles under a microscope; you need to know what it feels like to be a beetle."

When you empathize with your conflict partner, you listen to his emotions and respond to what he is actually feeling. "Walking in the other guy's moccasins" is an expression of what it means to empathize and to understand feelings. Empathy is non-judgmental. It doesn't matter whether you agree with your partner's feelings, only that you recognize that to him those feelings are valid and that you understand why.

The reflective statement is the tool of empathy. In its purest form, the reflective statement has three parts: an indication that you are making an observation (not a definitive statement); the feeling or emotion you're observing; and what the feeling or emotion is about. Of the three, the primary component is the description of the feeling.

- It sounds like you're *worried* that you won't get the report finished on time.

- I can see how *committed* you are to increasing market share.
- You seem *depressed* over the fact that you blew the sale.

In a way, when you make a reflective statement, you're guessing. Maybe I'm not depressed because I blew the sale, in which case I might say something like, "No, actually I was thinking over that last meeting, trying to figure out where I went wrong." If your guess turns out to be correct, I now feel free to open up to you and talk over how I'm starting to doubt myself because I not only blew this sale, but the last three as well. So in addition to making an emotional connection, reflective listening allows you to make sure your interpretation is right.

Some people are by nature problem solvers and have a tendency to jump into someone else's dilemma and try to fix it. But when your conflict partner is reacting emotionally, the worst thing you can do is try to deal logically with the problem. Feeling people need understanding, not practical solutions. You will defeat your purpose of understanding what it feels like to walk in your partner's moccasins to say, "You seem depressed about blowing that sale, *but* it's not that big a deal. Think of it as a learning experience." Or, "You seem depressed about blowing that sale, *but* if you had called the guy back when you said you would, things would have been a lot different." The "but" at the end of your statement will negate everything that goes before it, infuriate your partner, and put you right back into the conflict dance. By showing genuine compassion, you'll diffuse your partner's hostility and begin to nudge the pattern into a new shape. So when you get to the end of your reflective statement . . . STOP . . . and let your empathy hang, unqualified, in the air until you get a response.

Here are some examples of empathic, or reflective, listening.

- Jerry owns a small business that employs five people and

rises and falls with the economy. During a particularly tough period, Jerry had to cut costs in a dramatic way. Should he lay off an employee, and if so, which one? Or should he cut everyone's pay, including his own, until things got better? After a week of agonizing deliberation, Jerry chose the latter option and, in a highly charged meeting, broke the news to the group. The result was saddening, if somewhat predictable. One by one, the employees came into Jerry's office to find out what their cuts would be. Each in turn lashed out at Jerry, venting their anger in ways that stopped just short of accusing him of treachery. Jerry was devastated. He had tried to be fair and save everyone's job, but no one seemed to notice or care. Then the last employee entered the room, the one whose wages were the lowest and who had the most to lose. He sat down, folded his arms, and said quietly, "Jerry, this has to be the hardest thing you've ever had to do." Jerry never forgot the genuine understanding of that employee, and when times improved, he was lavish with his rewards.

- I had been calling a client regularly for some months to confirm a verbal agreement to conduct a series of workshops for his department and was having no luck in getting through to him. Finally, at 7:30 one morning he answered his phone. When he heard who was calling, he went off into a tirade. He was sick of having suppliers call every five minutes. He was overworked and had better things to do than arrange programs. He was angry and frustrated and just wished that I would go away. "Yes," I said, as gently as I could. "I can hear it in your voice." Willing myself to stay quiet, I waited through an interminable moment of silence. Finally, his voice came back on the line, apologizing for his outburst, thanking me for my patience, and inviting me to come in and sign a contract.

- Susan and her mother were at odds over who should be

invited to Susan's wedding. The guest list was too long, but every discussion of what names should be eliminated turned into a power struggle between mother and daughter and ended with Susan angry and frustrated, Mom hurt and upset, and no decision on makeup of the final list. After weeks of arguing, Susan made a move to change the pattern. She sat back in her chair, took a deep breath, and said kindly to her mother, "Mom, I know how excited you are about this wedding and how badly you want all your friends to be there. It's really hard for you to leave anyone out, isn't it?" Then she waited. No "buts" getting in the way. Just silence. Finally, Mom replied, "Susie, you're right. I *do* want everyone there, but I guess I've been forgetting that it's your wedding and you want your friends there too. What can we do about this?" And, bingo, they were able to settle down and work on the problem without the animosity that was spoiling the wedding for both of them.

To reflect means to listen with empathy and to respond to your conflict partner with understanding and compassion. You're not playing shrink here, condescendingly analyzing your partner's psyche. You're interpreting what you think are your partner's feelings and verifying your interpretation for accuracy. As with paraphrasing, be careful not to understate or overstate. To say, "Boy, you must be furious," when all you see is minor annoyance will make you seem phony.

One final *don't*. Don't say, "I understand how you feel." The response of your conflict partner will inevitably be, "The heck you do!" True empathy is not *telling* your partner you understand. True empathy is actually *understanding* and then conveying that understanding in a reflecting statement. Empathic listening is hard to do, but if you work at it, you'll be amazed at how your conflict will diminish in intensity and your relationships will improve over time.

Reflecting your partner's nonverbal signals

Earlier in this chapter, I said that one way to differentiate between the thinking and feeling responses of your conflict partner is to watch for mixed messages. When her words say one thing and her behavior says something else, you can be sure something emotional—something beyond the words—is going on, and you'd be unwise to ignore it. Freud said, "No mortal can keep a secret. If his lips are silent, he chatters with his finger tips; betrayal oozes out of every pore!" Because people often say what we want to hear, their words usually sound logical to us, and it's easy to let it go at that. Good listeners are always on the alert for nonverbal cues that tell the truth about what's really going on inside the other person.

"I can handle it," I respond when you give me a new assignment. Yet my shoulders droop slightly, I look pensive, and my voice trails up, asking a question instead of making a strong assertion. If you're watching (and watching is listening), you'll catch these signals and probe a bit further. "You don't sound like you're quite sure. Does anything about the assignment trouble you?" You've now opened the door for further discussion, and I don't feel like a foot dragger when I voice my concerns.

Louise told Mary she was thinking about applying for a position that had just opened up in the marketing department. "Wow," cried Mary, "that job would be perfect for me! You wouldn't mind if I applied for it, too, would you?" Louise froze. She minded terribly, but she put a brave (she hoped) smile on her face and replied, "No, of course not. The job's open to everyone." Mary got the job, and Louise never spoke to her again.

> Louise: *"It's not fair. She knew I wanted the job. She didn't care anything about our friendship."*
>
> Mary: *"I don't know what she's so mad about. I asked her if it was okay, and she said, "Fine, go ahead."*

If Mary had been listening (and watching is listening), she would have seen Louise freeze. She would have noticed that Louise's smile looked forced, and she would have probed further to discover what Louise really felt.

If her lips tell you, 'yes, yes,' but there's 'no, no' in her eyes, you'll be making a big mistake by assuming that either message is completely true. When you get a mixed message, you'd better check. Reflecting the nonverbal behavior of your conflict partner will help you do that.

Asking questions and using "tell me more" statements

Claire led the discussion with G-Corp by asking questions to check for accuracy. *You think we have duplicated our charges? Am I correct in assuming there are no other issues . . . ? Does it look that way to you?* These checking questions weren't intended to be manipulative or to lead G-Corp to unwittingly agree with Claire's position. They were honest queries for more information and to verify the accuracy of her assumptions. Once a point is agreed upon by both parties, you can go on to the next point without having to rehash old business ad nauseam.

Questions and "tell me more" statements also give your conflict partner a chance to give you more information. It prevents an immediate push-back to her push. Here's an example of the effective use of questions, "tell me more" statements, and reflective listening—all in one short scenario.

She: *You're always criticizing me. I can never do anything right.*

You: *I'm not sure what you mean. Give me an example.*

She: *Well, I cleaned my room and you complained there were clothes all over the floor.*

You: *Maybe you and I don't have matching pictures about what a clean room looks like. What does it look like to you?*

She:	*Well . . . it's dusted, and the bed is made . . . and the clothes are picked up.*
You:	*Do you think I'm being unreasonable by asking you to pick up your own clothes?*
She:	*You just don't understand.*
You:	*You're feeling very misunderstood right now. Let's talk more about that.*

If you can, avoid questions that begin with the word "why." *Why did you do that? Why are we leaving so early? Why are you wearing red?* "Why" questions are often complaints disguised as questions; and even if they're not meant that way, they could easily be perceived as criticisms by your conflict partner and put him on the defensive.

Questions and "tell me more" statements will give you greater insight into your conflict partner's thoughts and feelings. They open up a conversation in a nonthreatening, nonjudgmental way. You're not agreeing; you're not fixing; you're not defending. You're listening, and for now, that's quite enough.

Giving undivided attention

If you've ever tried to talk to someone who kept on doing something else, you know how maddening it can be. You may be hearing what your conflict partner is saying. You may be understanding and empathizing with every word. But if you don't *show* him you're listening, your efforts will be wasted. Even though you hear every word, you're not being a good listener if you clean out your desk, sign papers, or play computer solitaire while your conflict partner is explaining his side of the story.

The listening process isn't complete until your partner *feels* heard and understood. Quite simply, you must pay attention. So put down your other work (no matter how important you think it is) and concentrate on the conversation you're having—right now, in this moment. Sit quietly, with a relaxed, open posture. Don't drum on the table or shred paper clips. Watch what's going on, observing his non-verbal signals carefully for added meaning. Nod your head occasionally, and add vocal fillers like "hmm," "uh huh," and "go on," for encouragement. But use vocal fillers judiciously. I once worked with a man who sprinkled "uh huh's" between my every two or three words. Although he obviously meant well, I never thought he was really interested in what I had to say. Quite the contrary, I always felt "techniqued on," and his poorly timed fillers just about drove me crazy.

Too many rules?

If you're thinking there are a lot of dos and don'ts to this listening business—things you absolutely *must* say and things you absolutely *mustn't*—you're right. When you're dealing with the highly-charged emotions of conflict, volatility abounds. Both you and your conflict partner are in grave danger of overreacting, of exploding into heated argument and fortifying the very pain and anguish you're trying to extinguish. There's an extraordinary amount to think about, and a disciplined approach, together with care and caution, is required every step of the way.

In the heat of the moment, remember to stop, relax your muscles, take a deep breath, and think about your priorities. If one of your goals is to preserve the relationship, you must be gentle with your conflict partner and gentle with yourself.

Summary

Listening is not the act of hearing a few words and then launching into a lecture on why your conflict partner is so wrong-headed. Listening is hearing him out, accepting that in his own mind his point of view is valid, and making sure he feels heard and understood. This isn't easy, and you'll have to work at it, probably for the rest of your life. In addition, your desire to listen must be genuine, growing out of your heartfelt need to build a better relationship with your conflict partner. If he suspects you're faking it, he'll feel manipulated and the conflict will intensify, not lessen.

To listen well, you must first determine whether your partner is speaking logically or emotionally. If the words are overstated, the actions are out of character, or you're getting a mixed message of any kind, you can be pretty sure emotional issues are involved. Good listening requires becoming completely involved in the process, using tactics that include paraphrasing the content, reflecting your partner's emotions, reflecting your partner's nonverbal signals, asking questions and using "tell me more" statements, and giving undivided attention to your partner when he's speaking.

Listening is a skill. Understanding what's going on inside your conflict partner is an art, the mastery of which is invaluable and worth every bit of effort you put into it.

11

Step Five: Talk From Your Point of View

Up to this point you've been extremely patient. You've analyzed your conflict situation until you've understood it through and through. You've set some goals and determined your key priorities. You've stayed calm under the pressure of confrontation, and you've listened until you're about to pop. If you're like most people, your tendency all along has been to interject your own thoughts, welcome or not, into the conversation. You know you're right; you're convinced that *you* are the one who's misunderstood; and deep down you're terrified that if you don't get your oar in the water first, no one will listen to you. Now, after all this time, it's your turn.

Here's how it works. When your partner realizes you're really listening and making a genuine effort to understand her side, she doesn't have to fight anymore to get it across to you. Without being judgmental, you've already expressed her point of view—to her satisfaction. So she's better able to relax and respond in like manner to you. The key point to remember is that, while you listened from your conflict partner's point of view, you will speak from *your* point of view. You'll talk about *your* interests/needs, about how *you* feel, and what *you* plan to do.

Talk about your interests/needs

On Saturday mornings, my husband and I have a ritual. We drive (or bicycle in good weather) to the town of Jefferson, Ohio, near our home, for breakfast in the Jefferson Diner. We buy a newspaper next door at the newsstand and spend a pleasant hour or two over coffee, discussing current events and ball scores with other patrons, and getting our cholesterol fix for the week in the form of bacon, eggs, and home fried potatoes. One rainy Saturday in the car, we were half way to Jefferson when I made a discovery. Here's how the conversation went.

Me: *Darn it, I left my glasses on the kitchen table.*
Chuck: (smugly patting his breast pocket) *I have mine.*
Me: *Why didn't you remind* . . . (to myself: "Stop! It's not his fault you forgot your glasses. Talk from your own point of view, Carolyn) . . . *I guess I needed someone to remind me to bring my glasses.*
Chuck: *That's too bad. If I'd seen them, I'd have brought them along.*

So on we went to our usual pleasurable morning in Jefferson. Had I given in to my impulse to blame, Chuck would have defended my push with his own push back; we would have both gotten cranky, and the morning would have turned out much differently.

"I needed someone to remind me." is far less confrontational than *"Why didn't you remind me?"*. This is the essence of the statement that comes from your point of view. It offers your side of the story in the same nonjudgmental way that you received your conflict partner's. It opens with words like, *I need, I want, I expect, It's my hope that, It would be helpful to me if* . . . .

Periodically throughout this book, Brenda and Jane have popped in to illustrate a point. For Brenda to resolve her conflict with Jane in an assertive way, she must reflect Jane's point of view (that's the listening part) and then state her own.

> *Jane, I can see how pressured you feel when you have to get a big typing job out the door, and I'm happy to help you whenever I can. In order for me to support you and at the same time get my own work done, I need more lead time. If you can get the report to me 24 hours ahead of time, I won't have any problem helping you out. Can you do that?*

Now Jane has options. She can accept Brenda's offer, in which case expectations have been clarified and the conflict is resolved. Or she can say, "Gosh, Brenda, that's impossible. I never know when I'm going to get these jobs to do." And if she's smart, she will add, "But it's okay for you to say no if you're too busy. I'll understand."

When you talk about your interests/needs, it's not:

- *You're always late. You'd better get here on time from now on . . .* but perhaps. . . *We expect the people who work here to be on time, and we expect the same from you.*
- *You shouldn't do it that way . . .* but perhaps . . . *Here's an alternative method that I've found to be successful. I'd like to try it before we make a decision.*
- *We have procedures here that must be followed. You can't run off and do whatever you please. Your good intentions have just confused everything . . .* but perhaps . . . *If you have a great idea, I can back you up much easier if I hear about it from you before you take it to the committee. If you take me by surprise, I won't be able to give you my support.*

The basic message in each of these scenarios has remained the same, but the changed wording, even though still strong, has created a more cooperative environment. If your conflict partner feels free to choose an action, he will be more likely to stick with his commitment over the long haul.

If you force him to do things your way, you may win the battle over content, but his foot-dragging, backsliding, or (worse yet) sabotage will surely defeat you in the struggle over the relationship. What you're doing here is effectively eliminating the "push," so your partner can't "push back."

My friend from the last chapter who challenged the company's CEO with the message, "You require three things from me and I pledge them to you; in return, here is what I need from you," did exactly this. He respectfully stated his expectations and gave his new boss the opportunity to accept or reject his proposal. The CEO's willing agreement was a forecast of smooth sailing ahead. Had the CEO given a negative response, my friend would have recognized the potential for a troubled future relationship and made his decision about the new job accordingly.

Saying *I need, I want,* and *I expect* is extremely assertive behavior, because these words balance you evenly on the *Balanced Communicator*™ seesaw. You are firmly and decisively speaking from your point of view and at the same time remaining pleasant, tactful, and considerate of the viewpoint of your conflict partner. You are taking control of your personal power and giving up, once and for all, the roles of both victim and headbasher. The power of these words lies in their non-confrontational character and the fact that they give your partner choices. If you tell me I should do something, I can argue convincingly with you forever, because we're talking about me. But if you tell me you *want* me to do it, I have nothing to argue about. I can either do what you want or not, but the choice is mine, which makes us equal partners in the relationship.

In addition, when you're assertive about making your interests/needs clear, you remove the agonizing necessity for your partner to guess what it is you want.

She: *I'm off to the deli. Do you want me to bring you something?*

You:	*Gee, I don't know. What are you having?*
She:	*A roast beef sandwich.*
You:	*I don't much like roast beef.*
She:	*Well, ham's on sale this week. Do you want a ham sandwich?*
You:	*The ham usually has so much fat on it. I'm not sure I want that.*
She:	*Okay, what about turkey? The turkey's lean.*
You:	*I had turkey yesterday. What are you having again?*

If you and your conflict partner have conversations like this regularly, she will be ready for a screaming fit right about now. There are a number of possible assertive responses to her initial query, all of which make your wishes clear and move you closer to your shared goal of having lunch:

- *Hey, thanks, bring me a turkey sandwich.*
- *That would be great. Just bring me what you're having.*
- *I've been making decisions all morning and I'm brain dead, so bring me whatever's on special.*
- *I'm not sure what I want, so I'll take a raincheck this time. But thanks, anyway.*

By expressing both your conflict partner's interests/needs (that's the listening part) and your own, you're balancing the power between you. "This is what you're telling me you need from our relationship. This is what I need. How can we work this out?" You haven't patronized your conflict partner by belittling what's important to him, and you've been forthright in stating what's most important to you. You're moving slowly but surely toward collaborative problem solving, which we'll talk about in the next chapter.

Talk about how you feel

Another way to make strong statements from your point of view is to take ownership of your own feelings. It's so easy to give up power by putting the responsibility for your emotional well-being onto someone else.

- *You make me so mad.*
- *You're confusing me.*
- *I felt great until you squelched me with that remark.*

We are always reacting to what other people say and do; we don't live in a vacuum untouched by the words and deeds of those around us, nor would we want to. But we can, by taking ownership of our own emotions, limit the power others have over us. Besides, while expressing feelings seems to make us more vulnerable than we might like, it actually makes us stronger and keeps us safer. When you openly express your feelings, you accomplish two things. First, you lessen the power of your conflict partner to hurt you; in essence, you've pre-empted his attack on your hot buttons. Second, by exposing a usually hidden piece of yourself to your conflict partner, you make it easier for him to respond to you in a more open, less defensive way.

- *I was embarrassed when you shouted at me in the hallway this morning,*
- *I felt insulted when you left early yesterday, leaving me to clean up after the meeting.*
- *Participating in the conference is an important part of my career plan. I will be very disappointed if I'm not able to attend.*
- *The proposal reads well, but I'm worried that we're pricing ourselves out of the market.*

The tendency in the beginning stages of talking about feelings is to label every feeling one of *anger*. It's okay to express righteous indignation every now and then, but be aware that behind every angry feeling lurks fear.

- *I'm angry that you didn't get the report to me on time . . .* could really mean . . . *I'm afraid that I'll look bad to my superior and will be seen at upper levels as incompetent.*

- *I get mad when you discuss issues that concern me with the boss and leave me out of it . . .* could really mean . . . *I'm afraid I'm losing favor with the boss and will be shunted aside and forgotten.*
- *I get angry when you pick out the mistakes in my work* . . . could really mean . . . *I'm terrified that you'll discover I'm in over my head and shouldn't be doing this job at all.*

Anger is a secondary emotion that is generally kindled by fear. If, in your conflict situation, your pervasive emotion is that of anger, look beyond the anger to figure out what you're afraid of. Then, being as gentle with yourself as possible, see if you can express that fear to your conflict partner. This may not be easy for you to do. It entails taking what may seem to be a huge risk, which is precisely why speaking from your point of view is the fifth step in the conflict to compatibility process and not the first.

As with your listening statements, it's important to gauge the magnitude of the issue so you don't overstate or understate the intensity of the emotion. Mild concern is a long way from panic, so choose your words carefully. Some of the myriad of words that might accurately express your feelings are: "I'm feeling:

pleased	bothered	puzzled
glad	irritated	perplexed
happy	resentful	confused
confident	concerned	troubled
delighted	afraid	worried
excited	scared	depressed
eager	terrified	envious

One word of warning. Be careful that you don't hide a judgment statement behind the words *I feel.* I once counseled two women who were having trouble reaching agreement on how to manage a project. "No, no," one exclaimed to the other. "You just don't understand what I'm saying." I could see her partner gearing up for a push-back, so I quickly instructed the first woman to express what she was feeling. She thought for a moment and then said triumphantly, "I *feel* that you just don't understand what I'm saying."

Following *I feel* with words like *that, like,* and *as if* is a signal that you're expressing thoughts and judgments about the other person instead of your own feelings. In this case, a more appropriate "feeling" statement might have been, "I feel misunderstood," or "I feel frustrated because we're not connecting on this."

Here's another danger signal. When you begin a sentence, "I feel you should . . . ," it will be like waving a red flag in front of your conflict partner. Your moralizing can easily put her on the defensive, so avoid judgment statements like *you should* and *you ought to*, whenever you can.

Talk about what you plan to do

Lucy's son seemed to be in no hurry to finish college. He took the minimum number of courses each quarter, sometimes not even that, and in his third year he informed his parents that he had decided to take five years to get his degree. This bombshell precipitated months of bitter argument between mother and son . . . . Graduating within the normal four years would be a hardship. No, it wouldn't be a hardship if "you would just settle down and do some work for a change." Yes, it would. No, it wouldn't. Yes, it would. No, it wouldn't. Yes, it would; yes, it would; yes, it would!

Finally, Lucy performed a quick sidestep that changed the dance. "You know far better than your dad and I whether it will take you four or five years to finish school," she told her son. "And because we love you, we will continue to give you our moral support, no matter how long it takes. We will give you *financial* support for four years, so if you decide to take an extra year, you'll have to find another way to foot the bill. Keep us posted on what you decide to do."

Argument over. Decisions on how to run son's life transferred to son, where they belonged. The relationship is now more healthy, because it's based on clear expectations and mutual respect. What Lucy did was simply give a clear statement of her own intent, leaving her son's choices entirely up to him. He would now experience the natural consequences of his own actions, with Lucy remaining an interested and loving bystander. (P.S. Son finished school in four years after all.)

Please note that Lucy's statement was not a threat. She didn't say, "If you don't finish school in four years, we won't give you another cent." A threat is an attempt to coerce your conflict partner into taking an action that *you* want him to take, with punishment meted out by *you* if the action *you* desire doesn't take place. A threat hinders the development of cooperation. It may gain short-term compliance but will eventually intensify the conflict, because it creates an uneven playing field. You are now the aggressor and your partner has become the victim, a position that almost inevitably leads to retaliation. When you threaten, the push/push back syndrome goes on and on.

You'll go back and forth

You'll find that you'll weave back and forth between listening to your conflict partner and expressing your own point of view. In addition, be prepared to repeat yourself—patiently—until what you're saying sinks in. Here's a scenario that illustrates how this all fits together.

> You: *I'm finding a lot of mistakes on your expense reports, and I won't be able to reimburse you if they're not corrected.*
>
> Her: *Well, last time I wasn't able to get all the receipts. It wasn't my fault.*
>
> You: *It's easy to forget to ask for a receipt and it's a nuisance to have to be so careful. Just remember that I will send an improperly filled-out*

> *expense report back to you for correction before I pay it.*

Her: *Look, you can't do that. I need that money. It's not fair for you to hold out on me.*

You: *I know how frustrating it can be when you don't get reimbursed, and I want to make sure that doesn't happen. That's why I'm letting you know now that when your expense report isn't filled out properly, I will return it to you for correction.*

Think carefully before you make a statement about what you plan to do, because you must be prepared to follow through on it. Remember, your conflict partner is going to be uncomfortable with the new pattern you're trying to establish and will do her best to keep the old dance going. It's very easy to follow the path of least resistance and give in to the badgering of an aggressive partner. Keep repeating to yourself, "These are my interests/needs, this is how I feel, this is what I plan to do." Express your point of view as often as you must, always remembering to listen and reflect what's going on with your partner. Then follow through on what you say. Baseball players say they don't care if the umpire calls an outside pitch a ball or a strike, as long as he's consistent with the call. Your consistency in doing what you say you will do is part of being a *Balanced Communicator*™ and accepting the responsibility for the success of your relationships.

Check out your nonverbal signals

For two chapters, we've been examining what to say in order to move you and your conflict partner from conflict to compatibility. You've learned, I hope, how your mindful choice of words contributes to the betterment of your relationship. But we can't leave this subject until we consider very carefully the fact that it's not only what you say but how you say it that will move you forward. Your facial expression, your tone of voice, and your body language must all express caring, warmth, and a genuine desire to be collaborative. If you say, "I know you think this is a mistake, but I've gone over the figures and it still makes sense.", and your voice comes out in a condescending sneer, your conflict partner, having begun to open up, will shut right back down again, with her original opinion that you're a pushy know-it-all reinforced once more.

If you find you're getting negative reactions from what you think are positive overtures on your part, recheck not only your word choices but your demeanor. You may require some help on this, because we're seldom fully aware of our own nonverbal language. All we know is that people seem defensive around us and we don't know why. So ask someone you trust to watch you in action and point out to you those moments when your manner doesn't match your words. Remember, if there's a choice between words and behavior, your conflict partner will almost always go with the behavior, and your words, however well thought out, will be lost.

Build a reservoir of trust

At first, you may worry about goofing up, because there seems to be so much to remember. And it's likely that you will make mistakes, particularly at the beginning when everything is new and you're still experimenting with unfamiliar techniques. But if your partner feels you're sincere in your efforts to improve the relationship, she will give you some leeway, and your awkwardness and fumbling won't matter so much. You can also help your cause by building a reservoir of trust.

In talking to me one time about expense accounts, a sales manager compared two of his salespeople. "Joe is as honest as they come," he said. "If he lists an expense, I know it's legitimate, not a penny over. With Earl, I'm not so sure. He's been known to hedge, and I wouldn't put it past him to pad a bit."

Think about what this means. If there is ever a misunderstanding with Earl over expenses or anything else, suspicion will always feed the potential for serious conflict. With Joe, the manager will invariably give him the benefit of the doubt. Why? Because Joe, through his attitude and actions, has built up a reservoir of trust that can be drawn upon whenever necessary. Earl has allowed his reserve to become depleted over time, so people say, "Well, you know Earl. You'd better keep an eye on him." Earl will always start the ball game with a strike or two against him.

Your dealings with your conflict partner must be so open and so trustworthy that there is no doubt in his mind, or anyone else's, of your integrity and sincerity of purpose. If he has ever caught you in a lie (even an evasion of truth), or if you have done something that to him lacks integrity, you have poked a big hole in your trust reservoir, and you will have to work much, much harder to repair the damaged relationship.

If your conflict includes broken promises and lack of trust, and if you are the culprit, the time has come for you to be humble. Acknowledge your misdeeds, reflect your partner's feelings, apologize for your offensive actions, and ask what you can do to make amends. Then do it. This will clear the air and eliminate unspoken hard feelings. But it's only a start. Rebuilding trust takes meticulous, unrelenting effort over a long period of time.

A hidden agenda can hamper a relationship in much the same way as a dishonest act, because it creates suspicion about ulterior motives. In fact, in a close relationship, it's a mistake to harbor a hidden agenda; it will trip you up every time. So get your hidden agendas out in the open.

- *My decisions will always be made on the basis of what is best for the company. At the same time, I want you to know that money is important to me. So, while I won't jeopardize the company for my own personal gain, I plan to get rich while I'm here.*

- *I know that you want an atmosphere of teamwork in this office. That's difficult for me because I'm an independent, shoot-from-the-hip kind of person. I'm struggling with how to be a good team player and still hold on to my independence, which I think contributes a lot to what we're trying to accomplish.*
- *I am fully committed to my marriage and my family. Going back to school will fulfill my need to learn and grow as a human being, but will never take the place of my commitment to you.*

Open, honest discussion without fear, along with clear expectations and impeccable follow through, equals a harmonious living and working environment. We build our reservoirs of trust painstakingly—minute by minute, hour by hour, day by day, and year by year. When your reserve is full, the unintended mistakes you make in your relationships will be chuckled over and lovingly forgiven.

Summary

In addition to understanding the situation from your conflict partner's point of view, you'll need to learn to speak from *your* point of view. This means talking about your interests/needs, talking about your feelings and emotions, and talking about your future actions. This allows you to assert yourself in a nonconfrontational way, make your own choices, and leave your partner free to make his own choices. You are thus creating a more even playing field and communicating with your partner as an equal.

To ensure that both of you feel heard and understood, you will find yourself moving from speaking to listening and back again many times during a single conversation. Your choice of words is critical if you are to remain collaborative, with your nonverbal signals conveying your genuine desire to build a better relationship. Threats, blame, and condescending or patronizing mannerisms will only hurt your cause.

12

Step Six: Move to Problem Solving

An elderly couple wheeled their loaded grocery cart up to the checkout counter. She moved ahead of him to a spot beyond the bagger's station and out of the way.

He: *Get behind me so I can get the cart in.*

She: *I'll stand down here out of the way while you get in.*

He: *I said, get over here so I can get the cart in.*

She: *I'm not in your way. The coast is clear.*

He: *You can't help me there. Get over here and stand where I tell you.*

The checker at my counter grinned at me. "They're ninety years old and they've been doing this ever since I've worked here. Some people never learn, I guess."

This couple has been unable to move beyond the power struggle I witnessed in the grocery store because they are blind to the fact that they have a relatively simple problem—one that shouldn't be too difficult to solve. Restated as a goal, their problem is: *How can we best unload the grocery cart without getting in each other's way?* If they can resolve their differences on this issue, their relationship will improve. Yet ironically, their habitual power struggle over the relationship is blocking any effort they might make to

eliminate the problem and thus make their shopping trips—
and their lives—more pleasurable.

By now you're well aware that to insist on proving, once
and for all, who is right and who is wrong will dump you
and your conflict partner right back into blaming mode. At
this point, if you've been listening to your partner's point of
view and talking from your own, you have moved past all
that, and the level of trust existing between the two of you
has risen, at least temporarily. As the rhythms of your original dance begin to shift, you are beginning to understand
one another better. You're ready to explore in greater depth
the substance, or content, issues that have triggered the lat-
est flare-ups. You're ready to start solving problems.

Problem solving is not about who has power over whom
or who wins the argument. It's not about whether *my* way
or *your* way is the right choice, but how together we can find
a new and better way that satisfies as many of our individual interests/needs as possible and achieves a shared goal or
objective. As you work your way closer to compatibility,
keep in mind the idea of partnership. It is key.

Set an atmosphere of partnership

Most of the time throughout this book, I've used the
term *conflict partner* instead of *opponent* or *antagonist*,
because I've wanted to set a tone of cooperation rather than
coercion. So hold onto a picture of you and your partner
moving forward together to reach a common goal. Then talk
about your points of concern in terms of partnership, using
words that foster a spirit of teamwork.

- *You and I have had some disagreements over . . . .*
- *We could get a lot more done if we were able to . . . .*
- *You and I share a common goal. We can reach that goal
  together if we . . . .*

Think back to Chapter 3 and our description of the conflict between Sarah and Ken. The substance of their conflict was how they would allocate the resources of the marketing department for their company's greatest benefit. Their relationship was being damaged by Ken's interest in maintaining a position of favoritism in the eyes of the president. After having listened carefully to Ken's point of view and having expressed her concerns simply and without hostility, Sarah set the stage for partnering:

> *Ken, we've been disagreeing over what should go into this marketing plan. You've made some good points, and I appreciate your listening to my concerns. It seems to me that, instead of looking at this as an either/or proposition, we might be able to come up with a plan that includes the best of both our ideas. Then we can see what information we'll need to help us make an informed decision on exactly how to proceed. You know, my guess is that our boss is watching us pretty carefully to see how we get along, and this should show him how well we can do. What do you think? Can we work together on this?*

In this approach, Sarah accomplished a lot. She positioned the two of them as a team rather than adversaries, affirmed their common goal of creating a good plan, offered a concrete suggestion for how they might proceed, and planted the thought that, if they keep fighting over turf, they will both lose face with the boss. By remaining pleasant and understanding, yet firm in her resolve to successfully accomplish the task at hand, Sarah dealt directly with both the content and the relationship issues of the conflict. Because of the way Sarah structured her comments, it will be much easier for Ken to join in the spirit of collaboration. He really has nothing to lose.

Seek commitment from your conflict partner

Sarah did one other thing that will move the project forward. She asked for Ken's commitment by closing her remarks with the questions: *What do you think? Can we work together on this?* When Ken agrees, he will be ready to work toward a mutually agreed-upon solution. He and Sarah will finally have abandoned the philosophy that winning means forcing the other person to lose. The stage will be set for a joint triumph.

Freely given, a commitment from your conflict partner will almost always ensure cooperation. For example, Ben is a supermarket store manager who has tried almost everything, including threats, to get Marvin to come to work on time. In one form or another, Ben's arguments have gone something like this:

> *I don't see why you can't get to work on time. As a supervisor, you're supposed to be setting an example for everyone else, and you're letting the company down. You know what the policy is, don't you? Well then, if you're late again, I'm going to have to write you up.*

And Marvin invariably replies, "Yeah, yeah, I know . . . . Sure, whatever you say." The pattern is entrenched—Ben threatening and Marvin relentlessly nibbling away at the edges of the on-time policy. Ben will elicit a much more positive response by shaping the issue as a goal to be achieved, asking for a commitment from Marvin, and giving him the choice of either participating in the resolution or not.

> *Marvin, it's important to both of us that you succeed as a supervisor. One of your responsibilities is to set a good example for your department and, as you know, a key way to do that is for you to adhere strictly to company policy on punctuality. Recently, you've been*

coming in late, which isn't fair to the others. I
need you to cooperate by getting to work on
time. Can I count on you?

If Marvin agrees, he's honor bound to be punctual. If he continues to be late, he is saying, in essence, that being a supervisor isn't really that important to him, and Ben can act accordingly. His problem about what to do with Marvin will still exist, but its nature will have changed, and the repetitive conflictual incidents caused by unclear roles and expectations will have been eliminated.

One of the best negotiators I know always begins a session by reaffirming a common goal. "When we first got together," he will say, "we decided that we wanted to enter into a joint venture on this project. Are we still committed to that?" And if the answer is positive, "Good, then our disagreements will help to move us forward, not get in our way." Setting the stage in this way enables everyone to enter fully into the spirit of discussion, knowing that nothing anyone says will be misinterpreted or used against them.

Don't rehash the past

Earlier, on your own time, you painstakingly analyzed your conflict, so you have a good idea of its nature and how its patterns are likely to play out if you aren't able to resolve it. Don't make the mistake of replaying this analysis with your conflict partner. It would be all too easy for Sarah and Ken to fall back into the old argument over whose marketing ideas would win out. Or for Marvin to roll out his tried and true excuses in the vain hope that he wouldn't be held accountable for his lateness after all. Or for any of us to pontificate endlessly on why this didn't work and that didn't work and whose fault it was.

Our elderly couple in the grocery store are prime candidates for the "rehash" game. They could no doubt recite in detail over sixty years of hurts and insults, all intricately woven into their relentless "who's got the power" competition. Unfortunately, not a word would contribute constructively to the resolution of their conflict; indeed, the old stories would only arouse bad feelings and make things worse.

At times, we all take a perverse pleasure in revisiting old battles and re-experiencing old wounds. But at this point, don't allow either yourself or your conflict partner to fall into the trap of reliving the past. Stay in the present and look to the future. Keep yourselves firmly focused on what you're trying to achieve. *This is how you feel and what you need; this is how I feel and what I need; this is our common goal; now, how can we make it happen?*

Make lists

About to retire, Pete wants to sell the house where he and Meg have lived for forty years, but Meg is happy right where she is. Pete and Meg have argued passionately for months, and they have each enlisted friends and other family members for support. Sell! Don't sell! Their positions set, neither Pete nor Meg is willing to give an inch.

Meg: *This is my home. No other place would feel the same. I wouldn't have a garden. I wouldn't have enough storage space. The kids couldn't come at Thanksgiving because we wouldn't have enough room. I'd have to leave all my friends. I don't want to sell the house.*

Pete: *We can't spend money like we used to. This place is too big. It's too cluttered. It's got too much stuff in it. It's hard to take care of. We have to sell the house.*

Pete and Meg are making a mistake in assuming that their problem will be solved once someone wins the battle over whether to sell the house—that everything will then be all right and they can return to "normal." Selling the house may or may not be the best solution, but they can only discover this after they have restated the problem as a shared goal and determined what their interests/needs really are.

Using the goal, *to find a place to live that will satisfy as many of our individual interests/needs as possible, etc.*, Pete and Meg can now sit down separately and list what is important to them in a place to live. Pete's list might include: *ease of maintenance, expenses commensurate with my retirement income, fewer possessions so we can "unclutter" the place, etc.* Meg's list: *a yard of our own, enough space for family gatherings, a room to house my collectibles, etc.* They will note every possible idea; nothing is too insignificant to be added to the list at this time.

The next step is for each party to classify each item according to whether it is a need, a want, or a "nice-to-have." To determine the presence of a need, Pete and Meg must ask themselves, "How depleted as a human being would I be without this?" For most of us, a garden is something that gives us pleasure and we would like to have one; for a champion rose grower who lives for the time she's able to spend in the yard, her garden is a need she can't do without. If Pete and Meg are honest with themselves, they will each have one or two needs, many wants, and a whole bunch of "nice-to-haves" at the bottom of the list.

Now it's time to put the lists together side-by-side and compare them. But no editorializing, please. If Pete or Meg start poking holes in the each other's list, they will backslide into argument and somebody will end up mad. If the same item appears above the mid-line of both lists, it goes right to the top of a new list they will create together—a new list that contains all of their shared needs and wants, with the "nice-to-haves" as a secondary grouping to come back to.

With this master list in place, Pete and Meg can begin looking for living accommodations that meet as many of their requirements as possible. A lot of thoughtful discussion will accompany this process. *Is this really a need or is it a high-priority want? If this item on your list came to pass, I could probably get by without this one on my list. How important is this really to you?* Pete and Meg must continually remind themselves that their lists are equally important. They will gain more in the long run and their relationship will prosper if they give as much attention to the interests/needs of the other as they do their own.

Seek solutions in small steps

Often a major conflict is made up of many small arguments and disagreements, each feeding the bigger one until it's so huge it seems insurmountable. If you can break down your massive conflict into smaller more manageable pieces, the resolution of each piece will remove at least one obstacle to a lasting solution. This will enable you to work or live more comfortably alongside your conflict partner, since there will be one less issue to argue over day after day. Even more important, the resolution of a piece of your conflict will provide you with a small victory—one that will boost your confidence in a not-so-small way and will add immeasurably to your reservoir of trust.

For instance, the dispute between Sarah and Ken over the marketing plan is only one aspect of their larger conflict over their positions in the company and Ken's lack of trust in Sarah's motives. If they can put aside the bigger issues and work together on this one project, their winning plan will gain recognition for them both. Then, when Sarah makes no move to steal all the credit, Ken will come to realize that his own self doubts are a bigger threat to his advancement than Sarah will ever be. Each victory, however small, decreases the size of the overall conflict, and step by step, you'll make your way to a better relationship.

Brainstorm ideas together

Brainstorming is a way for two or more people to spontaneously generate ideas and is a valuable tool for finding creative solutions to many perplexing organizational problems. It can be equally as valuable in helping you and your conflict partner solve the problems confronting you in both your work and personal relationships. To brainstorm, see how many ideas you and your partner can generate that can move you toward your shared goal. Write your ideas down where you can both see them. Create a long list rather than a "good" list. In brainstorming, quantity counts, and the more items you have written down, the more possibilities for creative solutions will present themselves.

Initial judging of ideas isn't allowed in brainstorming. Let loose your imagination. Be crazy! The wildest ideas often turn out to be a stimulus for more realistic thinking and should never be discounted. Besides, laughter over goofy ideas can dispel tension and bring you closer together. Postpone voicing your opinions, both negative and positive, until your imaginative powers are exhausted and every idea is written down. When your list is complete, go back over it, item by item, exploring how you might be able to make each one work. Build on each other's ideas. Twist them, examine them from all sides, and turn them inside out, until gradually you begin to separate out those concepts that best fit your combined interests/needs. Sometimes, your plan will seem to unfold naturally, almost by itself.

The choice Pete and Meg will make about a place to live will be helped by a brainstorming session. Their present house may turn out to be exactly what they're looking for and, with a few adjustments in their lifestyle, they can live there happily for years to come. On the other hand, a condo in Arizona might provide them with more of their requirements. In any event, the list from which they select will be a comprehensive one. Selling the house, the cornerstone of their original conflict, is now only one of many possible choices and not the destroyer of an otherwise good relationship.

Brainstorming is a wonderful tool. It's creative, it's fun, and it works. Perhaps even more important, you and your conflict partner acquire ownership of all the items on your joint list. You won't have to argue over positions anymore. You can look objectively at the merits of each idea and study whether it can help you reach your common goal without fussing over who it belongs to. Because it generates new and creative ideas, brainstorming can, all by itself, help you interrupt the old patterns that have locked you in debilitating conflict. Used as part of an overall problem-solving process, it can set you more firmly on the path to compatibility that you thought possible.

Do it together

Unlike your initial conflict analysis, this problem-solving process is something you and your conflict partner must do together. Although your final conclusions may be ideal, if you have reached them on your own and tried to *impose* them on your partner, she will feel victimized all over again and will renew her efforts to dance the old dance. Your obvious dedication to making this a joint venture, along with your steadfast concern for her interests/needs, will reduce her defensiveness and go a long way toward ensuring her cooperation.

Often more information is required and, as it's gathered and weighed against each party's interests/needs, your objectives will either be supported or modified by the realities that surface. Under scrutiny, Sarah's early scheme to create new markets turns out to be more costly than she had originally thought and is dropped from consideration— without a word (or a gloat) from Ken. After lengthy deliberation over their combined needs and interests, Pete and Meg realize they can't make a final decision about where to live until they study *all* their options in greater detail. A trip to other sites grows out of their need for more knowledge, with Meg checking maintenance costs against Pete's budget and Pete on the lookout for space enough for Meg's garden.

All good problem solving leads to action, and the process in which you're presently engaged is no exception. Make sure, as you decide what to do next, that the action steps you agree on meet the following criteria:

- You and your partner must agree that the action step will contribute in some way to your common, or shared, goals. Pete and Meg's trip to potential retirement sites will result in greater knowledge about what options are available to them, and they will use this knowledge in making their final choice.
- Removing an item from your list must come as a result of an objective look at the facts of the matter and should be agreed upon by both parties. New information on costs brings Sarah to the realization that opening new territories is not a viable option, so she, reluctantly but with Ken's approval, initiates its removal from the plan.
- A decision must not clash with the interests/needs of either party. Meg wants space for her collectibles, but the final choice of a place to live must also allow for Pete's need for less clutter.

Summary

Problem solving is the final step in the move out of conflict into compatibility. It deals directly with the substance, or content, side of the conflict and, at the same time, protects the relationship by attending to the interests, needs, wants, desires, and drives of both you and your conflict partner. The key to good problem solving is keeping a "partnership" mentality and eliminating the idea that the other person is in some way your opponent, or enemy. Remember to:

- Seek his freely-given commitment to helping you find a way to make things better for both of you.
- Stay in the present and plan for a better future. Avoid rehashing the past and falling into a blaming mode, which will only perpetuate old patterns rather than establish new ones.
- Prepare a "wish" list of your needs, wants, and "nice-to-haves," and compare it with that of your conflict partner. Combine your individual lists into a joint list that takes

into account each of your highest-rated points. Pay as much attention to your partner's interests/needs as you do your own.

- If your overall conflict seems insurmountable and the relationship issues too big to handle, start small. By concentrating on a content issue and solving one small problem, you will establish a more trusting atmosphere. Additionally, the practice you get in managing the process itself will give you the confidence you need to tackle a larger piece later on.
- Together, brainstorm new and creative ideas and build them into a plan of action that moves you closer to a shared goal, one that doesn't clash with the interests/needs of either party.

13

What If It Doesn't Work?

Now you have it—the way to create the balance within yourself that will move you out of conflict into compatibility. A six-step process to deal with the issues over which you and your conflict partner are battling and to mend and protect an important relationship in your life. As you've seen, this process safeguards your interests/needs and requires that you do the same for your conflict partner. You are responsible for the success of each and every one of your relationships, and the closer the relationship the more effort is required on your part—effort that is part resolve, part perseverance, and part skill.

Earlier in this book, I said that you can't change the other guy. You can't make him do or be exactly what you want. You can only change the pattern of your behavior and, in doing so, invent a new dance that will be more satisfying to both of you. This means that when you begin this journey, you begin alone, without any guarantee of how things will turn out. You'll be saying to yourself, as so many others have: *I'm taking a big risk here. What if it doesn't work?*

The process is not a gimmick

The odds are with you. It's important to realize that this

method is not a gimmick—something that you try once and, if you don't get instant results, discard and go on to something else. Put to use over a long period of time, the *Six Steps to Compatibility* will become new habits, and one day you'll wake up to discover that permanent changes have actually taken place within you. You're not afraid of conflict any more, you're able to handle confrontation with greater confidence, and you've become a much better all-around communicator. Usually, your conflict partner will make a few brief attempts to return to the status quo and may even try to escalate the conflict for a period of time. But when he realizes you have a genuine desire to make things better and the changes you propose are to his advantage, he will gradually adapt himself to your new behavior and then to the new pattern that emerges.

Usually, that is. The situation may occur, however, where it becomes evident that your interests/needs and those of your conflict partner are truly incompatible. When you go back and reanalyze the conflict, you realize that, despite your efforts, he or she is unable or unwilling to meet you even halfway. Her desire to work independently conflicts with your goals of building an organization based on teamwork. His determination to keep the status quo interferes with your need to grow and change. The patterns are so ingrained that, in spite of your efforts, you can't break through the barriers, and certain scenarios play themselves out again and again:

He's too much of an old dog. It's said that you can't teach an old dog new tricks, and it's certainly true that the more entrenched some people are in their behavior, the harder it is for them to stop doing something one way and start doing it another. "It works for me," he says. "Why should I change?"

She's afraid of a level playing field. Your conflict partner may believe that she will be weakened if you become stronger. In this situation she will only feel safe if her position is one notch above yours (or anyone else's), and she is always jockeying for power, with every interaction becoming a game in "one-up-man-ship."

He's a cold fish. Your partner may not understand the important role emotions play in both professional and personal relationships. Refusing to even acknowledge the emotional side of the conflict, he coldly and logically hammers away at the content—in control and without compassion. Ironically, this response is often born of the fear of closeness, which paradoxically is in itself an emotional response.

She's a "lone wolf." Your conflict partner may be an independent worker who thinks cooperation, consensus, and other components of teamwork are a waste of time. Leave her alone and she can get the work done; ask her to collaborate and she resists.

He's playing by his own rules. He considers himself a "free spirit," comes and goes by his own clock, and isn't awfully concerned if you're inconvenienced. When confronted, he turns on the charm to smooth things over. He smiles, nods, and says, ". . . yeah, yeah, I know." Then he does exactly what he wants.

When you encounter unyielding resistance like this, it's easy to give it all up as a bad bargain. *I've tried my best and it didn't work. Oh, well.* Please don't make the mistake of letting the situation revert by default to its original pattern, the one you initially decided was unacceptable. Whenever you find yourself in an untenable situation, you have three basic choices. One, you can try to change the situation. This is what you've been doing throughout this book by taking responsibility for the success of your relationships and learning and putting into practice the *Six Steps to Compatibility*. Two, you can extricate yourself from the situation (and the relationship) and move on. Or three, you can learn to live with it and use your new skills to help you cope, biding your time until circumstances force a change and you can try again.

Getting out

If you can honestly answer *yes* to the question: *Have I done everything possible to resolve this conflict and create a more compatible relationship?*, and if the effort is draining and demoralizing you, it may be time to get out. In this situation, removing yourself bodily from the conflict is a perfectly acceptable option. You can ask for a transfer, get a new job, file for divorce, move to a new neighborhood, fire the s.o.b. Life is too short to spend a large percentage of it trying to protect a relationship that is clearly not going to work, and every now and then even the most compatible people decide it's just not worth the effort.

You're not obligated to spend the rest of your life trying to fix an unfixable situation; you have a job to do and a life to live, and it's time to get on with it. Besides, there are plenty of talented people out there who, given the chance, will become the compatible partners you're looking for, both at work and in your personal life.

When the time comes to let go of the relationship, you will know it. So make your decision and, with head held high, get on with it. One final time, tell your soon-to-be former conflict partner what you intend to do. But don't stop using the skills you've learned; stay balanced by dealing openly and honestly with the content issues . . .

- *No matter how we try, we don't seem to be able to agree on a marketing philosophy. You obviously need someone in the department who can support you and make your strategy work, and I'm uncomfortable in that role. The best thing for me to do is find a place where I can try out my own ideas.*

. . . and continuing to protect whatever relationship is left, by going easy on your conflict partner . . .

*This has been a good place to work. You have
treated me well, and I hope you feel the company is better for my having worked here.
Please call me if I can help you in any way.*

Learning to live with it

Realistically, however badly you may want to walk away
from your conflict, you may not be in a position to do so. In
this case, reframing the situation—looking at it from a new
perspective—can often ease the pressure of too-high expectations on both parties and open the door to a workable, if
not preferred, resolution to the conflict. Are you looking to
someone for friendship at work who doesn't believe in making friends with fellow employees? Do you want understanding from a conflict partner who, at least at this point, is
incapable of showing empathy? Are you asking for blind
obedience from a child who is struggling to become independent? There are times when an adjustment of expectations will prevent a relationship from going completely sour
and keep you from feeling that you're helplessly beating
your head against a wall. Here are some examples:

- Kyle expected Leonard, his new business manager, to
  become a partner in the firm after he had learned the
  business. He discovered that, while Leonard understood
  the financial end of the business very well, he didn't have
  the temperament for managing people that his firm
  required. Kyle's attempts to educate Leonard in his new
  role as a "people person" were met with a resistance that
  soon degenerated into conflict. Kyle had to realize that,
  while it was okay for him to be *disappointed* in Leonard's
  lack of people skills, he could no longer hold out the
  expectation that Leonard would in time become partner
  material. He reduced his own expectations, became comfortable with Leonard in the permanent role of business
  manager, and looked elsewhere for a new partner.

- To make ends meet while she went back to school, Leslie took a job as an X-ray technologist in an urgent care center. It didn't take her long to discover that she was *not* working in a compatible organization. The environment was rife with conflict and people weren't very nice to each other. Leslie's expectation that she would be spending her time in a congenial, supportive atmosphere had to be quickly revised. Her strategy became: *go to work, be pleasant to everyone but avoid involvement in the conflicts, do a good job, go home, and use the money to pay for school.* Accepting a more realistic picture of what her workplace was like instead of holding onto the expectation of what it *should* be like enabled Leslie to work her way through school in a harsh environment without hard feelings or heartaches.

When you make the choice to live with a situation, you do so consciously and not by default. In essence, it's a strategic choice that is accompanied by a **resolve not to complain**. A teenager accepts that, as long as she lives at home, she will have a 12:00 midnight curfew. She stops whining, is never late, and on her eighteenth birthday moves into her own apartment where she can set her own hours. Without griping, a manager patiently puts up with an underproducing employee until a replacement can be found. Cramped in tiny quarters, an entire office staff bites its collective tongue and remains cheerful in spite of the chaos caused by fast growth and slow cash flow. Admittedly, these are stopgap measures, but they go a long way toward relieving tension and getting away from constant unpleasantness.

Keep on keepin' on

Whether you're trying to change the situation, removing yourself from it, or learning to live with it, whatever you do, don't stop the process. Keep it going, no matter what, because you're on the right track. The *Six Steps to*

Compatibility are a way of life, not a gimmick. Keep them in your mind as a checklist, choosing and making use of the step that's most appropriate at the moment. Let's take a moment to review the steps.

1. *Analyze the conflict*. Look again at the patterns. You may be surprised to find that small changes are occurring and you're actually getting results.

2. *Reexamine your goals and priorities*. Check to see if they're still realistic, recommit to them if they're on track, and adjust them if necessary.

3. *Stay calm under pressure.* Take a deep breath, relax your muscles, and stay open. Tell yourself over and over again that you are in command of your reactions and that you can handle any confrontation that comes your way.

4. *Listen carefully.* Paraphrase, reflect, and pay attention. Remember that, although you're striving to understand your conflict partner's viewpoint, good listening does not require agreement on your part, only comprehension.

5. *Talk from your point of view.* When it's your turn, share your thoughts, your expectations, and your feelings with your partner. Without threatening, talk candidly about your own actions. Continue to switch back and forth between talking and listening, watching for your partner's responses and soliciting her feedback. You're still seeking common ground, not trying to convince her of the rightness of your position.

6. **Use the "partnership" approach to problem solving.** Be gentle with your partner and with yourself. Continue to affirm the value of your relationship, yet be relentless about solving your problems in ways that allow you both to win.

Conclusion

When you take responsibility for the success of your relationships, you take charge of your life. *You* decide what you're going to say—and do—and be. When your partner joins you in collaboration and helps you form a new and increasingly satisfying alliance, magic happens in the relationship. If he chooses to remain outside your circle, that is his choice and his loss. Your dance will go on very nicely without him.

In this book, I've attempted to give you a new way of relating to other people—one that will make you stronger and more confident in your dealings with friends, family, and colleagues. The next step is yours. And as you take it, let these famous words be your guide:

I'm not in this world to live up to your expectations,
You're not in this world to live up to mine.
For I am I and You are You.
And if we choose to find each other it will be beautiful,
If not, that is our choice.

Appendix

Once you have an understanding of and practice in each of the *Six Steps,* you can draw on them, singly or in groups, whenever you need them. On the following page, you'll find a diagram of the pathway to compatibility, as it's most often played out.

- As soon as you recognize you're in conflict with someone, turn to *Step 1.* As part of your analysis of the conflict, determine if it's predominantly substance (content) based or if there are significant relationship issues involved. Remember, if you're having the same argument over and over, or if you're *always* fighting with your conflict partner over something, your conflict is, at least in part, one of relationships.

Substance based?

- If your conflict is substance based, move directly to problem solving *(Step 6).* In cooperation with your conflict partner, put *Step 2* into practice by sitting down together and determining your joint goals and priorities.
- Make continual use of *Steps 3, 4,* and *5.* Keep your cool, listen until you understand, and talk from your point of view—over and over and over again—until you reach a conclusion that satisfies you both.

Relationship based?

- If you decide the relationship is important, you'll have to work on that right away. Move to *Step 2* and set your own personal goals and priorities.
- Weaving *Steps 3, 4,* and *5* in and out of your conversations, clarify and mend your relationship with your con-

flict partner and gain a commitment from him to work together on the problems that face you.

• Now you can move to problem solving *(Step 6)*, set joint goals and priorities, and proceed as above to a joint solution.

THE PATHWAY TO COMPATIBILITY

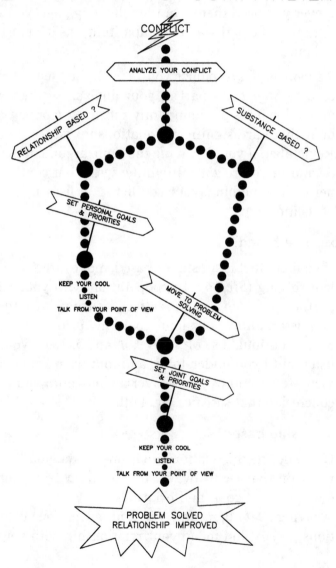

About the Author

Carolyn Dickson is founder and president of VOICE-PRO Incorporated, a leading business communication consulting firm headquartered in Cleveland, Ohio. A nationally sought-after speaker and coach, she has helped thousands of business professionals, including top corporate CEOs, from leading firms across the country become better speakers, presenters, and all-around communicators—thus more successful and responsive leaders.

To receive further information about the programs and services of VOICE-PRO, or to arrange for a speech or presentation by Carolyn Dickson, or to order additional copies of *Creating Balance* or *Speaking Magic,* please contact:

VOICE-PRO Incorporated
2055 Lee Road
Cleveland, Ohio 44118

Phone: 216-932-8040
              1-800-261-0104
Fax: 216-932-5048

INDEX

D

dance, 4, 6, 27–28, 31, 35, 38, 46–47, 49, 52, 88, 104, 106, 112, 120, 123, 130
deep breathing, 68. (see breathing, diaphragmatic)
denial, 21. (see conflict, styles)
detachment, 41–42, 63
determine your goals and objectives, 35. (see Six Steps to Compatibility)

E

Encyclopedia Britannica, 37
expectations, differing, 18–19, 82

F

feelings
    ownership of, 101
    words to describe, 103
Fisher, Roger, 87
flexible yet consistent, 27. (see *Balanced Communicator, The*)
"flight or fight" response, 65
focus, 53, 66, 69, 73
force, 23. (see conflict, styles)

G

Getting to Yes, 87
G-Corp, 82–85, 92
goals
    and priorities, table of, 61
    value of, 53
"Great Humiliator, The", 86

H

Henry Higgins, 18
homeostasis, 37
"hot buttons", 65, 102